Contents

▲

Preface

The U.S. Small Business Administration esti-
mates there were more than 16 million self-employed people in
the United States in 1999, the latest year for which data is available. You could become one of them by following the advice in
this book.

Whether you're ready for a career change, you're
tired of working for someone else, or you're just interested in
making a few extra bucks every month, a lawn care service business is a viable way to achieve your goal. There's plenty of work
for even a new business owner in most parts of the country. The

initial investment in equipment and the monthly overhead is fairly low. Plus the pay is great—and you get lots of fresh air and exercise while you earn it.

While this book contains all the advice and tips you need to be successful in the green game, you *won't* get instructions here on how to mow lawns, sculpt magnificent topiaries, or winterize your weedwhacker. Those are basic skills you need to develop on your own—either by practicing on unsuspecting clients' lawns or by studying turf grass basics at your local community college. What you will get, however, is a solid background in what it takes to run a successful business. Because although you may not realize it now, you need to be a pretty shrewd businessperson in addition to a mowing maven to make this whole gig work.

For instance, you have to know how and where to find new clients because clients = work = taxable income (which will of course be of particular interest to Uncle Sam). You have to know how to balance your books and develop sideline businesses to keep yourself busy when the snow gets too deep to trim the rose bushes. And you have to know how enough about turf and weather conditions in your part of the country to become a true Grass Master.

Here's a sampling of the major topics covered in this book:

- Estimating lawn size and setting your price
- Deciding which lawn care services to offer
- Determining who and where your best customers are and how to market to them
- Setting up a viable business structure and naming your fledgling business
- Writing a business plan (and you thought all you needed was a riding mower and good weather)
- Finding the right business professionals to advise you
- Selecting the right lawn maintenance equipment, vehicles, and supplies
- Hiring employees as your business grows
- Learning from industry gurus, trade associations, and other sources
- Conquering the mysteries of the Internet and harnessing its power to grow your business
- Determining the cost of doing business and managing your finances

You'll also find stories and advice here from successful lawn care business owners from around the country that can help give you the confidence you'll need to make your fledgling business work.

Does this sound like just the job for you? Then, gentlemen and ladies alike, start your engines and let the mowing begin!

The Green, Green
Grass of Home

When you think back to the long, lazy summers of your youth, chances are your recollections are full of achingly nostalgic memories like an oversized tire swing under a big shady tree. Tall frosty glasses of lemonade wreathed in pearls of moisture. Crickets and tree frogs throatily singing

Photo ©PhotoDisc Inc.

their sweet night song. And the high-pitched whine of lawn mowers carried on the warm summer breeze.

If you're like a lot of people, you were trudging along behind one of those mowers back then, pushing with all your might and sweating profusely, just so you could make a few bucks to buy some baseball cards or a really cool bike. You may have occasionally mowed down a few pansies or zebra-striped a lawn, but you sure were proud when the homeowner came to the door, surveyed your handiwork, and forked over the agreed-upon fee.

Mowing lawns for a living will give you that same sense of pride—while earning you some pretty serious cash.

The Green Scene

There are many advantages to running a homebased lawn care service. You're master of your own destiny, and you can devote as much or as little time to the business as you want. You have a short commute to work if you're based in your own community. You can work at your own pace and at virtually any time during regular daylight hours. You also can enjoy the fresh air, get a good cardiovascular workout, and bulk up your muscles.

Do You Have the Right Stuff?

Ask yourself these questions to see if you have what it takes to become a successful lawn service owner:

○ Are you motivated enough to work without a bear of a boss breathing down your neck?

○ Can you resist driving your sit-down mower over to the park for some R&R on beautiful summer days?

○ Do you have the stamina to slather on sunblock regularly and spend a lot of time under the blazing sun?

○ Are you fairly nimble on your feet so one day you won't accidentally find yourself under the lawn mower mentioned above?

○ Can you tell the difference between turf and Astroturf in a blindfolded test?

○ Can you develop a viable sideline business to support any unbreakable habits you may have (e.g., paying the mortgage, buying groceries, etc.) during the winter?

○ Do you know what the keys numbered 0 to 9 on an adding machine are for?

○ Can you keep your four-year-old from answering your business telephone line with "Hi, can you come over and play?" during working hours?

○ Are you willing to wear a personalized company T-shirt in colors that blend tastefully with your mowing equipment?

○ Are you willing to work long hours in the hope of earning big bucks?

Total your "yes" answers. Scoring:

8–10 = Congratulations! You are truly the Blade Master.

4–7 = The force is with you. Work hard and prosper.

1–3 = It's a good thing you bought this book.

0 = Maybe you should try a career in floral design or culinary arts instead.

The price of all this freedom and body contouring is relatively low—so low, in fact, that many new lawn service owners use their personal credit cards or small personal loans to fund their new businesses. Once you invest in the tools and toys you need to manicure lawns professionally, you're generally set for years. You don't need much in the way of office equipment, either, and you can set your office up in a corner of the den or a spare bedroom rather than laying out extra cash for a commercial space.

Reality Check

This all sounds pretty appealing, doesn't it? But of course, every Garden of Eden has a serpent, and a lawn care business has quite a few of its own coiled up and waiting to strike. To begin, you have to be a lot more adept at mowing, trimming, and pruning than the average person. That means you'll have to invest some time in learning gardening basics and techniques. You'll have to be a disciplined self-starter who can ignore the call of a glorious spring day and diligently service your clients rather than heading for the lake or golf course. You have to be physically fit and able to handle the rigors of the job, which can include lifting heavy equipment off and onto trailers, and wielding bulky handheld implements for hours at a time. You'll be handling potentially dangerous machinery and hazardous chemicals. And you'll have to be a very savvy business manager who can administer cash flow, invent advertising and marketing campaigns, and implement a survival plan that will take you through the lean winter months.

But even with such obstacles, it is possible to prosper in this industry. In the chapters ahead, we'll show you how to lay the groundwork to start a thriving lawn care service. We'll cover day-to-day responsibilities and the various tasks integral to running this type of business. We'll also touch on the myriad issues a new business owner will face, such as tax, insurance, and financing matters. But perhaps best of all, we'll share advice and words of wisdom from successful lawn care business owners who have made their personal dreams of prospering in a business they love come true.

Industry Snapshot

Before we get into the nitty-gritty basics of running a professional lawn care business, let's take a look at the industry as a whole and the opportunities it presents for aspiring entrepreneurs like you.

According to a recent lawn care operators study conducted by Maritz Marketing Research Inc., there are an estimated 10,000 individual lawn care service providers in the United States. These run the gamut from independent operations to franchises and divisions of large corporate chains. It's believed that the number of businesses could actually be significantly higher because there are so many people doing lawn maintenance informally and on a cash basis. What is known for sure, according to the Occupational Outlook

Stat Fact
According to a recent Gallup survey, the average annual amount spent by consumers on lawn and landscape maintenance was $508.

Handbook 2000–2001 (U.S. Department of Labor), is that two out of every ten landscaping, groundskeeping, nursery, greenhouse, and lawn service workers are self-employed and provide maintenance services directly to customers on a contract basis.

The market they serve is huge. A Gallup survey sponsored by the Professional Lawn Care Association of America (PLCAA) and several other green organizations indicated the U.S. lawn care market, which includes lawn and landscape maintenance, landscape design and maintenance, and tree care serv-

Fun Fact

According to the Gallup Organization, the top things consumers look for when choosing landscape and lawn care professionals include: good references and reputation, satisfaction guarantees, free estimates, longevity, local ownership and operation, and insurance and bonding.

ices, grew to $17.4 billion in 1999 (the latest year available). Factor in the lawn and garden supply category, and the industry was worth $21 billion in 2000 (the latest year available), according to a study conducted by research company Packaged Facts. What's more, it's expected to grow to $26 billion by 2005.

Who's fueling such phenomenal growth? The 77 million aging baby boomers, many of whom are affluent homeowners. They recognize the value of a well-kept lawn, but they often don't have the time or the inclination to do the maintenance themselves.

"Year after year, lawn and landscape maintenance continues to be the top service hired by homeowners," says Tom Delaney, executive vice president of the PLCAA. "Homeowners benefit from the economic and environmental benefits of turf, and save time by hiring a lawn and landscape service. When you factor in that a well-maintained property can add anywhere from 5 to 15 percent to a home's value, you quickly realize that hiring a service is a sound investment."

That's where you come in. By offering the right mix of services, you can clip off a neat little piece of this business yourself. Exactly how much can you earn? The sky's truly the limit. The lawn care service owners we interviewed for this book earned anywhere from $9,000 to $50,000 in their first year, and as much as $160,000 to $250,000 once they were in business a few years. They offer services ranging from basic mowing and trimming to landscape maintenance and chemical application. And none of them has more than five employees!

It's possible for you to achieve this kind of success, too. So turn the page and let's get started.

2

Turf
Talk

If you've been mowing lawns all your life, you already know the basic technique. But did you know that even though a carefully sculpted lawn appears to be beautiful and healthy after being mowed, the mowing process itself is actually bad for all those little green plants? That's because when you mow, you're essentially scalping each tender blade, a process that removes a part of the plant that's used for photosynthesis. If you remember anything about botany from high school science classes, you know that's the process plants use to turn sunshine and nutrients from the soil into the sugar, starch, and cellulose that allows them to thrive. That's why it's not a good idea to crop grass too short during the regular mowing season—you could severely damage those food-making machines. It's also why the experts recommend that you mow often (at least once a week) and remove no more than one-third of the blades each time.

Luckily for our lawns, today's mowing technology is much more sophisticated and less damaging compared to the clipping techniques of yesteryear. Until around 1830, people used scythes, those wicked curved blades that are swung in an arc and take out anything in their path. As you can imagine, it was pretty hard to get an even trim that way. Then Edwin Budding, an English textile engineer, realized that the device he invented for shearing the nap on fabrics might work on grass. But it wasn't until the early 1900s that the first gasoline-powered mower debuted—and changed the process of mowing forever. Now you can just stroll along and let the mower do the hard work, or climb into the driver's seat and put the pedal to the metal. Of course, all this power will cost you (we'll get to that in Chapter 6), but it also means you can do a lot more mowing in a much shorter time (translation: you can make more money faster).

Business Basics

As you know, lawn maintenance is a seasonal business, with downtime during the winter in about two-thirds of the country. Depending on your area and climate, the prime growing months run from about April to early October. You'll need to market your services aggressively in the spring so you'll have enough clients to carry you through the summer. Then, in the fall, you should be winterizing lawns, raking leaves, and collecting past-due accounts. Still have energy left to spare? Then during the winter, you can offer services like snow plowing. If you decide to take a well-deserved break instead, you'll have to make sure in advance that you've budgeted wisely throughout the year and have sufficient funds to carry you through those income-free months. (We'll discuss finances in Chapter 12.)

The typical start-up lawn care business services 20 to 30 residential clients a week and offers up to three types of services: mowing, fertilizing, and chemical application. For the purpose of this book, we'll focus on mowing and fertilizing, since chemical applications (herbicides, pesticides, and fungicides) are a whole industry unto themselves. It's also a closely regulated industry that requires practitioners to earn certifications that permit them to handle hazardous materials. Most lawn care service owners prefer to start out with basic mowing and add other services as they become more experienced and acquire more equipment.

Grass Attack

Basic lawn maintenance consists of mowing, edging, and trimming. Often, bush and hedge trimming is offered as an extra service, but it's more time-consuming and requires more manual dexterity than mowing. Lawn businesses sometimes send out two people to a job site so one person can do the mowing while the other edges and trims the areas the mower can't reach. But if you're a one-man band (or one-woman band), you'll just have to allot extra time on each site to complete both jobs. Fortunately, not all lawns have to be edged every time you mow. Sometimes only minor touch-ups are necessary, which you can do using a hand edger.

It's crucial to the survival of your business to keep all your equipment in peak working condition. That means cleaning the mower blades at the end of each day and using a grinding wheel regularly to keep them sharp.

> ### Smart Tip
> *Tip...*
>
> Sizing up the competition is an important part of the due diligence you need to do before you launch your business. Check the Yellow Pages to see who's offering what services, whether it's discounts to seniors or add-on services you haven't thought of.

You should also use a balancing weight to prolong engine life and to help prevent white finger, a form of Raynaud's disease caused by exposure to constant vibration from equipment like lawn mowers. Clean oil and air filters regularly to keep engine wear to a minimum and improve performance. The oil should also be changed often—as much as once a week, since the high heat of the mower causes lubricants to break down fast.

It goes without saying that you should take every precaution to protect yourself while working. Always wear safety goggles and ear protection, and always remember to let your mower cool down completely before you gas it up. Because the cutting blade can rotate at up to 200 miles per hour, never put your hand into the discharge chute or turn the mower over while the blade is spinning. In addition to the obvious injuries it can inflict, that razor-sharp blade can catapult projectiles like rocks, metal, or even compacted grass that can do a body some serious damage.

> ### ⚠ Beware!
>
> Anytime you work with gasoline-powered equipment, there's always the possibility of sparking a fire, especially in brush country or areas experiencing a drought. Carry a fire extinguisher rated for multiple uses, and make sure your mowers have spark arrestors.

Spreading the Wealth

If you choose to include fertilizing in your business mix, you'll need a drop spreader. Be sure you practice with it before attacking a customer's lawn, since you can

▲

easily burn or unevenly treat the grass, resulting in an unsightly mosaic of sickly green and yellow patches (and the loss of a customer, no doubt). Another option is broadcast spreader which will disperse the fertilizer over a wider area (thus saving you time) but can provide less consistent coverage.

Always clean out your spreader well at the end of the day because fertilizers are very corrosive and can damage the hopper.

"Guesstimating" Your Worth

Another important part of the job is providing estimates to prospective clients. Unfortunately, this is an inexact science, at best. Most of the owners Entrepreneur spoke with "guesstimate" how much time it will take them to mow a homeowner's property, then multiply that by a price per hour. The problem with this method is that land features like slopes and ornamental landscaping can affect the price. For example, let's say it will take you 70 minutes to mow a 10,000-square-foot property using a 22-inch mower. But toss in a backyard that's landscaped with driftwood and rocks and has a raised vegetable garden, and your estimate is no longer quite as accurate.

A Dynamic Duo

There are only about two dozen types of grasses that thrive in North America, according to the Web site yourgrass.com. Each is climatically suited to the following regions to assure a perennial crop.

- ○ *Cool/humid zone* (covering most of the northern states and some of the Midwest): Kentucky bluegrass, fescue, ryegrass, bentgrass, zoysiagrass
- ○ *Warm/humid zone* (the Southeast and southern part of Texas): Bermuda, zoysiagrass, carpetgrass, centipede, bahiagrass, St. Augustine
- ○ *Warm/arid zone* (Southern Texas to Southern California): Bermuda and buffalograss in the most arid parts of the zone
- ○ *Cool/arid zone* (the drier parts of the Midwest and West): cool-season grasses like Kentucky bluegrass and tall fescue, buffalograss
- ○ *Transition zone* (the Central United States): zoysiagrass, tall fescue, Kentucky bluegrass, perennial ryegrass (in the northern most part of the zone), Bermuda (in the southern most part of the zone)

"Estimating is definitely the hardest thing about this business," says Rick Q., a lawn service owner in Temecula, California. "I go with my gut feeling a lot, so if there's a formula, I want to know it!"

Experts recommend pricing based on lawn size. It's less arbitrary to set up a pricing structure this way, plus you'll seem more professional to your prospects if you have an established, formal price structure. You can compensate for unusual land features by building an extra amount—say 10 percent—into your price.

One thing you never want to do, Rick Q. says, is to "blind bid," or do an estimate without visiting the property personally. "If you blind bid, then you're a fool and should get out of this business," he says bluntly. "I once bid on a property from hell that hadn't been maintained for two years, and if I hadn't gone over to see it first, I would have lost my shorts."

Bidding in person has another advantage: You can pitch additional services at the same time. "I always try to sell fertilizing, aeration, power mowing, and other add-ons when I do an estimate," says Mike A. in Renner, South Dakota. "But I do use a soft-sell approach—if someone is already getting the lawn fertilized and doesn't seem interested in having me do it, I never push it."

Establishing Prices

Before you can make an estimate, you have to know how much to charge per square foot. Since the lawn care industry is so competitive, it's important not to overprice your services. So a good way to figure out how much the market will bear is by calculating the size of your own lot and calling a few of the lawn care companies in the Yellow Pages for an estimate. (Typically, owners of lawn care services calculate their prices based on the total square footage of the lot. They can usually estimate roughly how much of a lot is landscaping.) Then recruit a few family members and friends to call for quotes on their lawns, too, so you can get a feel for prices on lots of different sizes. This will help you determine the acceptable price range in your community, and then it's easy to figure out where to price your services. This method works especially well if you're doing business in a community with uniformly plotted subdivisions or other similarly sized lots.

Incidentally, while you don't want to be the most expensive service in town, you don't have to undercut the competition to get jobs, either. Pricing your services somewhere in

Bright Idea

If you're still not sure how much to charge, add up your family's living expenses for the year. Then add in your business expenses. Divide that figure by 1,920, which is the average number of working hours per year. The result is the minimum hourly rate you need just to make ends meet.

the middle or toward the top of the range is a good rule of thumb. Then it's up to you to demonstrate that your professionalism, quality service, and reliability set you apart from the competition and justify a higher price than the cheapest kid on the block.

Here's another easy way to calculate your fee: Ask those same friends and family members who helped you out by calling your competitors how long it takes them to mow their own lawns. That will give you an idea of the time necessary to mow lots of various sizes. Then use this formula:

$$\text{Estimated cost of labor} + \text{\$25 per hour} = \text{Your rate per cut}$$

You can play with the $25 per hour cost, but what it should reflect is your overhead costs (such as phone, office supplies, advertising, equipment, vehicles, etc.) and supplies (like gasoline and trash bags for yard waste removal).

Applying this formula, here's how you would estimate a 10,000-square-foot lot that takes 55 minutes to mow:

$$\underset{\substack{\text{Est. Labor Cost} \\ \text{(1 Hour @ \$9/Hour)}}}{\text{\$9}} + \underset{\text{Cost Factor}}{\text{\$25}} = \underset{\text{Suggested Rate}}{\text{\$34}}$$

We used a labor cost of $9 here because the Occupational Outlook Handbook 2000–2001 (U.S. Department of Labor) says that the median hourly wage for landscaping and groundskeeping laborers is $8.24. You can round your estimated labor figure up or down as you see fit and according to what your local market will bear.

Armed with all this information, you'll want to create a pricing schedule sheet that you can refer to when you're asked for a quote. We've provided a sample on pages 15.

When you actually are asked for a quote, ask the homeowner for the dimensions of his or her lot as a starting point. If the prospect doesn't know, you can use a measuring wheel, available at any home improvement store, to measure both the frontyard and backyard of the property. If the land isn't a perfect rectangle (which is often the case), you can make some rough adjustments for the irregular shape. And don't forget to carry a supply of estimate forms and a measuring wheel in your truck at all times. You never know when you might have an opportunity to bid on a new job.

The owners interviewed for this book charge anywhere from $20 to $85 per cut. Others charge a flat rate like $100 per month or $40 per hour. All of them base their estimates on a visual inspection of the property, and some measured the mowing area as described above.

So far, we've been talking only about residential lots. You can apply the same formula to commercial properties. It bears mentioning that it can be harder to land commercial accounts, especially when you're new in the business and haven't built a reputation yet. But it never hurts to try bidding on commercial work, which can be done for everything from golf courses to office and condominium complexes, business parks, and municipal parks.

Ken W., who lives in Armada, Michigan, a rural community, has a single commercial account as the centerpiece of his business—and what a lucrative account it is. He mows and trims the local cemetery, a job that takes him four to five days a week twice a month. He also pours cement for headstone foundations (the little platforms the headstones sit on so they don't heave or shift) and services 13 residential clients.

"The cemetery job pays well, so I don't need a lot of customers," says the retired General Motors employee and part-time lawn service owner. "I've always landed new business through referrals, and over the years, my customers have become more like friends."

Landing a commercial account like Ken's can be challenging, but not impossible. First, call the company you're interested in working for and ask to be put on its bid list. Then you'll be notified when work comes up for bid. You also can take a more proactive approach and send a sales solicitation letter directly to the company and hope for the best. (You'll find a sample letter in Chapter 9.) Of course, you'll need property measurements to determine a rate before you send the letter.

The rates charged by the lawn service owners interviewed for this book varied widely, but all charged by the week.

Start Your Engine

Of course, the actual lawn care you do will be the single most important part of your regular business day during the summer. But you also will have to attend to numerous other details to keep your business running smoothly.

To begin with, part of your time will be spent scheduling jobs. If you only have half a dozen or fewer clients, a written schedule isn't necessary. You can probably keep track of your clients in your head. But when you go above that level—and certainly when you acquire ten clients—you need a formal schedule to keep organized. In addition, with gas prices heading farther north all the time, you should service all clients located in roughly the same area on the same day, if at all possible. Clustering mowing jobs this way also keeps you from wasting valuable time crisscrossing your market area.

Smart Tip

To avoid fatigue, schedule regular breaks during the workday. Also, even in the early stages of establishing your business, limit the number of hours you work each week. Your productivity will slip and your enthusiasm will erode if you push yourself too hard.

You can easily create a simple schedule using a columnar pad available at any office supply store. There also are a number of scheduling software programs just for lawn service companies that you can try (they're discussed in Chapter 6).

Another part of your time will be spent advertising and marketing your services. Most of this effort should be done in the spring, right before the start of the regular mowing season. But from time to time, you'll hear about an advertising opportunity too good to miss, like buying an ad in a recital program for a dance school in an affluent area, or sponsoring a Little League team. You'd then have to spend time creating a new advertising piece. (We'll talk about advertising strategies in Chapter 9.)

Finally, general office administration will take up a chunk of your time. This will include returning phone calls, handling the finances (i.e., accounts payable and receivable), giving instructions to employees, rescheduling work hampered by weather, and sending out invoices. As far as the latter is concerned, there are two ways to handle invoicing. First, you could leave a preprinted invoice inside the customer's screen door or rubber banded to the knob. It's not necessary to speak to customers at all, and in fact, they will probably appreciate that you didn't interrupt them just to hand over a bill. Don't leave your bill in the mailbox. It's considered private property and it's illegal to use it for anything other than mail delivered by a USPS carrier. You can keep a book of invoice forms (available at office supply stores) in your truck and handwrite the bill at every stop.

Second, you could generate your invoices at the end of the month and mail them all at once. This will necessitate stuffing envelopes and spending money on postage, but sending a bill through the mail gives the impression that you're a professional who takes the business seriously.

Pricing Schedule

Square Feet	Mowing	Fertilizing
1,000	$29	$18
1,500	30	18
2,000	31	19
2,500	32	19
3,000	33	20
3,500	34	20
4,000	35	21
4,500	36	21
5,000	37	22
5,500	38	22
6,000	39	23
6,500	40	23
7,000	41	24
7,500	42	24
8,000	43	25
8,500	44	25
9,000	45	26
9,500	46	26
10,000	46	27
10,500	47	28
11,000	48	29
11,500	49	30
12,000	50	31
12,500	50	32
13,000	51	33
13,500	52	34
14,000	53	35

Pricing Schedule, continued

Square Feet	Mowing	Fertilizing
14,500	$54	$36
15,000	54	37
15,500	55	38
16,000	56	39
16,500	56	40
17,000	57	41
17,500	58	42
18,000	59	43
18,500	60	44
19,000	60	45
19,500	61	46
20,000	62	47
20,500	62	48
21,000	63	49
21,500	64	50
22,000	64	51

3

Mowing Down
the Competition

Now that you have a good idea of exactly
what a lawn service operator does, it's time to lay the groundwork for creating an efficient and successful business. The place
to start on the quest toward establishing your business is with
market research.

Market research is necessary for several important reasons. First, it helps you identify exactly who might be interested in using your services. Second, it helps you determine whether the area where you want to set up shop can actually sustain your lawn care business. Finally, it provides you with useful information and data that can help you avoid problems down the road that could negatively impact your business (that is, problems that could put you out of business).

You might be thinking, "Whoa! I'm an aspiring lawn technician, not a statistician. Besides, people have lawns everywhere. There's bound to be enough business in my area to keep me busy."

Maybe, maybe not. The lawn care industry may have generated annual sales of $17.4 billion in 1999, according to the most recent Gallup survey, but not every part of the country has the same need for lawn care professionals. Take, for instance, those parts of the Southwest where the ground cover consists mostly of scrub, rocks, and lizards. Unless you're planning to install lava rock or cacti, it's a safe bet that a traditional lawn care business is going to die on the vine. Likewise, even in states like Washington and Oregon, where rain is abundant and the grass gets as high as an elephant's eye, it's possible to have an overabundance of lawn care services in a particular area.

The best way to find out about these kinds of shortcomings—as well as potential opportunities—is by researching your target market. Fortunately, this is something you can undertake yourself even if you don't have a background in statistics or research, according to David L. Williams, Ph.D., an associate professor of marketing research at Wayne State University in Detroit.

"With the exception of questionnaire development, which can be difficult for a beginner to do well, you can pretty much handle all the research yourself on a reasonably small budget," Williams says. "The problem is, many small-business owners view market research as an optional expense. But it's the only accurate way to find out what's important to your customer."

This chapter will show you how to find out who will use your services, learn where they live and work, and determine the kinds of services they'll want you to provide. Armed with this information, you'll be able to make informed decisions that can help your business grow and prosper.

Defining Your Audience

Who is the typical lawn-care customer? If you had to come up with a simple formula for defining your target audience for a lawn care business, here's what it might look like:

Homeowners + Grass = Potential Customers

If only it were that simple. But the truth is, there's a lot more to starting this kind of business than gleefully buying mowers and power tools, printing up business cards, and waiting for the phone to ring off the hook. You have to study the demographics of the area you wish to do business in carefully so you can tailor your services to a specific niche within that market.

Demographics are the characteristics of the people in your target audience. These characteristics may include age, education and income level, gender, type of residence, and geographical location.

According to a recent survey by Lawn and Garden Trends, a number of demographic groups spent more than the national average on lawn care. They include: homeowners 30 to 49 years old, men, people with professional occupations, people who are college-educated, married couples with children, people with annual incomes of more than $50,000, and people in both the suburbs and small towns.

That takes in a lot of ground, so to speak, but if you look closely, you'll see there's a lesson to be learned. To apply it, start by looking at the community where you want to establish your business. Maybe you live in a college town that's overrun with hale and hearty 18- to 20-year-old men. Maybe you live in a small town where the average wage is $20,000. Or maybe you live in a condo-heavy area.

Maybe you should find somewhere else to set up shop. But you'll never know for sure unless you conduct an organized market research study.

Conducting Market Research

The goal of your market research is to touch base with potential customers to find out whether they'd be interested in using the services of a lawn care business, as well as exactly what types of services they may require.

There are two kinds of research—primary, which is information gathered first-hand, and secondary, which is information culled from external sources. Each has its own merits as well as costs.

Primary Research

The most common forms of primary research are direct mail surveys, telemarketing campaigns, and personal interviews. Assuming that you'll want to save your start-up

Mission Possible

Understanding your market and the people you'll serve is critical to the success of your business. But understanding yourself and defining exactly what you plan to do is equally important. So follow the lead of America's most successful corporations and write a simple mission statement that includes your company's goals and outlines how you will fulfill them.

A typical mission statement for a lawn care service might say "Jim's Mowing and Power Raking will serve the needs of busy urban professionals by providing basic mowing services and power raking. My goal is to land 15 weekly mowing customers in the first six months of operation."

Here's another possible approach: "Lush Lawns is a full-service lawn care provider that offers more services than the other three area competitors combined. Courteous, prompt customer service, as well as knowledge of and certification in the application of chemicals, are the hallmarks that will distinguish this business, and allow it to achieve sales of $50,000 in calendar year 200x."

And here are some actual mission statements from owners *Entrepreneur* spoke to:

○ "We're building our reputation one yard at a time." (Mike A., South Dakota)
○ "To give a value added service to our customers so they keep us and become a valuable part of our business." (Chris B., Texas)
○ "Treat everyone's property like it was our own." (Rick Q., California)

Your mission statement is your compass as well as the foundation on which your future is built. It can be one sentence long (as in the case of Pepsi's mission statement—"Beat Coke"), or it can be several paragraphs. The length doesn't matter; the direction it provides is what's important.

capital for equipment and advertising, you should probably try a survey first since it's the most cost-effective way to gather information. You also should do the survey yourself rather than hire a market research firm, because that can be quite expensive.

Your survey should be no more than one page, since it's difficult to get busy people to fill out anything lengthier. The questions should be well-phrased so they're direct, clear, and unambiguous. They also should be constructed so the information they gather is useful and conducive to analysis. For example, a question like "Would you be interested in hiring a lawn service?" isn't very useful

Mission Statement Worksheet

Here's your opportunity to try your hand at writing your own mission statement. Begin by asking yourself the following questions:

❏ Why do you want to start a lawn care business?

❏ What are your personal objectives? How do you intend to achieve them?

❏ What skills do you bring to the business that are useful and beneficial?

❏ What is your vision for this business? Where do you think you can take it in one, two, and five years?

Using this information, write your mission statement here:

Mission Statement for (your company name)

_____

_____

_____

_____

_____

_____

_____

_____

_____

_____

_____

because it's closed-ended, meaning it's possible for the respondent to give a yes or no answer without elaborating. That's not going to give you much insight, which is the whole point of this exercise.

Although you could draft the questions yourself, you should consider asking someone experienced in market research for help. Since market research firms tend to be pricey, Williams of Wayne State University suggests contacting the business school at your local university instead. A marketing professor on staff might be willing to draft your questionnaire for $500 to $1,000, or may even assign your questionnaire as a class project free of charge, as Williams himself has done. You'll also find a market research letter and questionnaire on pages 23 and 24 that you can use as a guideline.

Surveying the Market

This part is easier than you might think. Start by purchasing a mailing list that's targeted to the market you wish to reach. Local homeowners associations, list brokers, and even daily newspapers in major metropolitan areas can sell you a list of heads of households that can be sorted in many ways, including by ZIP code so you can target a specific geographic area. (You can find a huge listing of publications that sell their lists in the *Standard Rate and Data Service* directory, published by VNU, which can be found in many large libraries.) Some other criteria you're bound to be interested in will include occupation (if you're looking for homeowners with professional jobs), gender (since men are the primary consumers of lawn care services, according to *Lawn & Landscape* magazine), income (the more money someone makes, the more likely he or she will be willing to pay for lawn care), and age (especially middle-aged people and senior citizens). Need another list source? Try the *Directory of Associations* (Gale Research), which can be found at most large libraries.

Once you have your list in hand (which is usually priced as a flat rate per 1,000 names), you're ready to produce your questionnaire. To keep the cost down, use your home computer to create your own letterhead, and format the questionnaire, then stop by a quick print shop like Kinko's and have it photocopied.

Another good source of lists is consumer home and garden shows. The organizations that run these trade shows usually compile the names of attendees for their exhibitors. You may be able to purchase a copy of the list directly from the trade show organizer. You'll find a list of some of the largest lawn care industry shows in this book's Appendix.

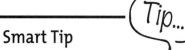

Smart Tip

Compiled lists are lists of names that have been culled from published sources such as telephone directories and organization rosters. *Hot lists* consist of the names of known buyers, and are usually taken from magazine subscription lists, mail order buyer lists, and so on. Hot lists cost more to rent, but are worth the cost because the information is usually fresher and more accurate.

Cash as Bait

How would you like an easy way to improve your response rates? Try enclosing a crisp, new dollar bill with your survey. The dollar is sent as an advance token of thanks to the recipient for taking the time to fill out and return the questionnaire. Although it doesn't guarantee a response, the buck certainly is an attention-getter, and direct marketing studies have shown that sending even a small cash honorarium tends to improve the rate of return.

Market Research Questionnaire Letter

Pterodactyl Lawn Service
5555 Park Avenue
Lincoln Park, Michigan 55555

July 5, 200x

Mr. Rainer Shine
5555 Penny Lane
Plymouth, Michigan 55555

Dear Mr. Shine:

I'll bet after a long day at work, you're ready to stretch out in your recliner with the newspaper or the remote control, and just relax and unwind. What you probably don't want to do is to spend a big part of your evening or weekend trying to whip your lawn into picture-perfect shape.

That's where I can help. I'm about to launch a lawn care service in the metropolitan Detroit area to take the burden off people like yourself who want a beautiful, healthy lawn, but have limited time to care for it. So would you please take a few minutes to answer the enclosed questionnaire to let me know if you might be interested in lawn care services?

Thanks for your help.

Mike Kairis, Owner
Pterodactyl Lawn Service

Of course, this trick could cost you a pretty penny, so to speak, since, according to Williams, surveys should be sent to a sample of at least 300 people to yield useful data. However, a sampling of even as few as 100 surveys would be useful and would only require a $100 investment if you choose to include a monetary incentive. You could also offer respondents a discount on your services.

Calling All Lawn Owners

Telemarketing is a highly effective, if time-consuming, way to gather information. As with surveys, you'll need a strong telemarketing script with questions similar to those on

Market Research Questionnaire

1. What is your age? ❏ 18–29 ❏ 30–45 ❏ 46–60 ❏ 61 and up
2. Which of the following lawn services might interest you? (Check all that apply.)
   ❏ Weekly mowing, edging, and trimming
   ❏ Hedge trimming
   ❏ Tree trimming
   ❏ Fertilizer application
   ❏ Pest control
   ❏ Winter snow removal
3. What is the maximum you'd be willing to pay for basic mowing service?
   ❏ $25 per week ❏ $40 per week ❏ more than $40 per week
   ❏ Other (specify) $ _____ per week
4. Do you currently use a lawn care service?
   If no, would you consider using a lawn care service at this time?
   ❏ Yes ❏ No
5. What is your household income? ❏ $25,000–$40,000
   ❏ $41,000–$55,000 ❏ $56,000–70,000 ❏ $71,000 and up
6. What is your educational level? ❏ High school diploma ❏ College degree
   ❏ Graduate school degree
7. What is your profession? _____

If you would like to be contacted by a lawn care service provider, please provide your name and phone number here: _____
Thank you for your time.

your market research questionnaire and a good prospect list. But when you call, don't just fill out the form. Listen carefully to the person. He or she is bound to make comments and have concerns about things you never even considered. That helps you add to the storehouse of knowledge you'll tap into when you're ready to go after your first clients.

A Job for the Pros

If you're really nervous about doing your own market research and you have a sufficiently large start-up budget, you could hire a market research firm to help you.

These firms are located in most large cities and will be listed in the Yellow Pages. Not only will they collect the information for you, but they'll also handle all incoming data and will analyze the results and prepare a report for your review.

Williams says a smaller shop might charge you $2,000 to $3,000 to handle a survey project for 100 people and prepare a simple report. The cost for 200 to 300 market research interviews and a report would be about $4,000 to $8,000. But since that can take a pretty big bite out of your start-up budget, seriously consider doing your own research before turning to the pros.

Secondary Research

> **Beware!**
> Mailing lists are purchased for one-time use. Lists are "seeded" with control names so the seller will know if you use the list more than one time. If you wish to use the list more than once, you'll have to ante up again.

If you're looking for real cost savings when doing market research, try using secondary research. Someone, somewhere has probably researched something that relates to what you want to know, and you can often get your hands on that information free of charge.

The mother lode of statistical information can be found at state and federal agencies, since they collect data on everything from income levels to buying habits. Although this data may be a year or two old, it can still be very useful, particularly for the fledgling lawn business owner who doesn't have a lot of money to spend on research. Some great sources of information are the U.S. Census Bureau (www.census.gov), the Small Business Administration (www.sba.gov), local economic development organizations, and even utility companies, which often have demographic data they'll provide free of charge or for a very nominal fee.

Other sources of useful secondary research include your local library, chamber of commerce, state economic development department, trade associations, and trade publications. You can find the names of thousands of trade publications in the Standard Rate and Data Service directory.

> **Bright Idea**
> Visit your market area's county seat to obtain copies of census tracts, which give population density and distribution figures, as well as reports on population trends over the past 10 years. Study the communities carefully for signs of declining, static, or small populations, since they're not likely to be hotbeds of new business prospects and may best be avoided.

Economic Environment

Dollar Stretcher

Try to keep the market area you serve within about five miles of your home (or office, if you go that route). Driving longer distances is costly in terms of time lost, money spent on gas and maintenance, and extra vehicle wear and tear.

Before we move on, there's one more very important factor to consider in your market research efforts. That's the economic base in your prospective market area.

Depending on what's happening with the national economy, a lawn service may be considered more of a luxury than a necessity. So it's up to you to convince your prospective clients that they need your services because it will make their lives easier.

If you've done your market research right, you already have some idea about the average income levels in your neighborhood. Now you need to look at data such as the percentage of people who are employed full-time and the types of jobs they hold. If the local market is driven by a lot of blue-collar, heavy-industry jobs, a downturn in the economy could make cash tight and affect your ability to keep customers. So could a plant shutdown or a scaling back of local services. A call to your city's economic development office is an easy way to get a handle on the health of local industry.

The Cream of the Crop

Upper middle-class homeowners who hold white-collar jobs and own homes on 4,000- to 7,000-square-foot properties are usually the ripest prospects for lawn care services, even if they already use a lawn service. They could be unhappy with the level of service they're currently receiving and would be receptive to a quote from you.

Be on the lookout, too, for new subdivisions with estate-sized lots that are being built in your market area. Put on a company shirt and a dazzling smile, and make a point of visiting the new homeowners shortly after they move in—even if they don't even have their sod and landscaping installed yet. The landscaping company that lays the sod may have its own lawn maintenance division and certainly will make a bid to care for the lawn after the installation job is completed. So you'll want to make your own bid as soon as possible, since it's likely to be lower than that of an established landscaping business and thus may look very tempting to a cash-strapped new homeowner.

While you're at it, ask about the area's white-collar jobs since these people are your best prospects, as well as the types of companies that support them. You also need to make sure you have a backup survival plan if you aspire to serve an area that's heavily dependent on a single industry.

Chris B. in Tyler, Texas, is one lawn service owner who studied his market carefully before deciding to expand his lawn chemical services into a second market area. "My partner and I looked at demographics carefully because we were primarily interested in serving dual-income families with kids who had a minimum salary of $50,000," Chris says. "We figured these were our most likely prospects because they were busy and would want to enjoy their family instead of working on their yards."

It was a good call. The new business is now growing nicely, thanks to door-to-door marketing efforts and postcard mailers.

Your Budding
Business

Just like grass seed needs nutrient-rich, fertile

soil in which to grow, your lawn care business needs a formal

legal foundation to ensure compliance with commonly accepted

business practices. This chapter discusses standard operating

procedures for everything from practical legal issues to

business insurance, and shows you how to get your business machine oiled, cranked up, and ready to run.

Naming Your New Baby

Choosing a name for your company should be high on your list of priorities in the early stages of business development. Many lawn service owners opt to use their own names combined with a business description, like "Ed's Lawn Care" or "Mark Lindsay Landscaping." There are a couple of advantages to this kind of name. Naming the business after a real person (that's you) can make the business seem more credible and reliable. It's also beneficial because many people like dealing with a company owner. So unless you have an unpronounceable name like "Zbrecz Gazorninplatz," feel free to toot your own horn and name the business after yourself.

If you decide to use your own name, be sure to open a business checking account right away so you can keep careful records of business deposits and expenditures separate from your personal transactions. Otherwise, you could run into trouble at tax time because the folks in Washington may have trouble distinguishing between your personal income and your business income.

There's at least one good reason *not* to use your own name as part of the company name, though. Let's say one day you decide to sell your business because you won the lottery and decide you want to mow lawns just for fun. It could be hard to sell a business named "Greg Charalambopolous Lawn Wizardry" to a guy named Joe Smith, especially since part of the value of your company name is the recognition it has in your market area.

Steve M., an owner of a lawn care business in Mendota Heights, Minnesota, has been grappling with the problem of name recognition since 1998, when he bought a full-service lawn care business that had been around for a decade. In his case, the previous owner's name wasn't part of the business name, but the positive reputation that he wanted to perpetuate did ride along with the business moniker.

"I'm still not sure I like the name, but other people seem to," says Steve. "I've been going back and forth about changing the name, but it's familiar to other people and it's catchy, just like you want a business name to be."

Smart Tip
Business checking accounts at large banks may come with hefty service fees. To find a small business-friendly bank, call around and compare fees before depositing your hard-earned cash. Another way to tell if the bank will appreciate your business: Visit www.entrepreneur.com/best banks for a state-by-state listing of the nation's small business-friendly banks.

Dollar Stretcher

If you have access to the Internet, you can do your own no-cost name search. Start by checking for nationally registered trademarks on the U.S. Patent and Trademark Office Web site at www.uspto.gov. You can also search for names using popular portals like America Online, Yahoo!, Google, and Lycos. Network Solutions (www. networksolutions.com) can also tell you if there's a Web site that uses the name you've chosen.

Steve's right. Catchy, creative names that identify who you are without being too cute can be great attention-getters. But be sure to stay away from names that are too over-the-top, like "The Green Guy," "The Brawny Lawnman," or "Lawn Shark" (definitely too much like "Loan Shark"). Not only are overly cute names not very professional, but they won't inspire confidence in your clientele, either.

Nathan B., an owner in Sykesville, Maryland, learned this lesson firsthand. When he started his business as a teenager, he had a young man's enthusiasm for the wacky and fun. So he named his business "Yardvark," a deliberately misspelled variation on "aardvark." As both he and his business matured, he realized a name change was needed.

"I always got a lot of grief from customers, and after a while, even I started feeling foolish answering the phone 'Yardvark!' every day," says Nathan. "The name just didn't have a professional, commercial sound."

So Nathan eventually gave the business a name that has a more solid, dependable connotation.

By now it should be obvious that you should take your prospective business name out for a spin before you print up your business cards and other business documents. Have a friend call you a few times so you can answer the phone using the new name. It should roll off the tongue easily (just imagine saying, "Leonard Wisniewski Reliable Lawn Care" a couple dozen times a day). Be careful, too, if you pick names that use alliteration ("Steady Stu's Lawn Service") or use words that are hard to distinguish over the phone ("Tuck's Sod and Stuff").

And speaking of building name recognition, there's another simple little trick you can use when selecting a name that can put your business in the spotlight immediately. Selecting a name that starts with an A or another letter toward the beginning of the alphabet can put you first in the phone listings, which is helpful since people tend to start at the top of the listings when using a phone directory. Of course, not everyone can be listed in that coveted first spot (although some people just keep adding A's to their designation—like AAAAAAAA Lawn Service—to keep a stranglehold on first place), but you can choose a unique name that's distinctive and evocative of what your business does. To help you get started, check the Yellow Pages for ideas (as well as to avoid duplication), then use "The Name Game" brainstorming form on pages 39 and 40.

▲

Once you've picked a suitable name, it's time to move on to the next step: setting up your business structure.

Registering Your Corporate Name

Most states require you to register your fictitious company name to ensure it's unique. This is usually done at the county level and is known as filing a dba ("doing business as") statement. The fee to file is usually nominal (around $30 to $60) and entitles you to use the name for a limited period of time—usually three years. When the time expires, you simply renew the dba. Before you get your dba, however, a search is done to make sure your name is unique. If you happen to choose a name that's already being used, you'll have to pick something else, so it's a good idea to have a few names in reserve.

Incidentally, adding words to your name automatically makes it a fictitious name and means you must register it. The good news is, unless you have a very common name (like John Smith), chances are it's unlikely to be in use already.

Your Corporate Structure

Once you've registered your dba, you are considered to be the proud owner of a legitimate business. So naturally, the IRS will have something to say about the way you run it. (You knew we'd get around to the IRS eventually, didn't you?) Basically, this means the bureaucrats in Washington require that you operate as one of four business entities: a sole proprietorship, a general partnership, a limited liability company (LLC), or a corporation.

Sole Proprietorship

Most lawn care professionals choose to operate as sole proprietors because it's the easiest type of business to form. All you have to do is file a dba as discussed above, then open a business checking account in that name. You can use your personal credit card to pay for business expenditures if you want, yet you still get tax benefits like business expense deductions. But there is a downside to the sole proprietorship. You are personally liable for any losses, bankruptcy claims, legal actions, and so on. That can wipe out both your personal and business assets if you're ever sued by a customer. (Good liability coverage is a *must* in this business. See Chapter 5 for a discussion of insurance options.)

General Partnership

If you're planning to join forces with another entrepreneur to open a business, you are forming a general partnership. Partnerships are easier to form than corporations, and you don't have to file any documents to make them legal. But since each partner is responsible for the actions of the other, it's a good idea to have an attorney draw up a partnership agreement that spells out exactly what each person is responsible for.

Limited Liability Company

A third type of business entity is the limited liability company, or LLC, which combines the tax structure of a partnership with protection from personal liability. This type of partnership is a little less common among lawn care business owners but can be useful if you want some added protection for your personal assets.

Corporation

The last type of business arrangement is the corporation. It is established as a totally separate legal entity from the business owner. Establishing a corporation requires filing articles of incorporation, electing officers, and holding an annual meeting. Again, not many lawn care professionals choose this route initially because the costs are prohibitive and the company must pay corporate taxes. On the other hand, owners of a corporation will find it easier to obtain financing for things like buying big-ticket equipment, building a storage facility, or buying property to put that storage facility on.

Chris B., a chemical lawn treatment business owner in Tyler, Texas, believes a corporation is the way to go when teaming up with a partner. "We formed a corporation to protect our assets, pure and simple," he says. "It only cost $300 to set it up because I did all the paperwork myself, and it really wasn't that difficult to do."

Stat Fact
To incorporate a business, you must be at least 18 years old. In some states, you have to be at least 21.

Incidentally, if you operate under your own name, you can use your social security number when filing your business taxes. But if you adopt another name for your sole proprietorship as discussed earlier, or form a partnership or corporation, you are required to have a federal employer identification number (EIN). To apply for an EIN, pick up a copy of form SS-4 at any IRS office, or print one off the Web site at www.irs.ustreas.gov You'll also need a dba, as discussed above.

If you're not sure which business arrangement to choose, you should talk to an attorney experienced in handling small-business issues.

"There are advantages to each kind of entity, and an attorney can help you decide which one is best for your situation," says attorney Daniel H. Minkus, chairman of the business law section of the State Bar of Michigan and a member of the business practice group of Clark Hill PLC. "If you don't know the people you are doing business with, I'd encourage you to form a single-member LLC or corporation. They're simple to create, and they're invaluable because your clients are dealing with your enterprise, and not you personally."

You can incorporate without using an attorney, just like Chris B. did. The forms are fairly easy to fill out, and it will cost you $50 to $300 to do it yourself, vs. $400 to $1,000 if you have an attorney handle the process. But corporate law is complex, so it may be a better idea to allow a professional to handle this for you.

You'll find information about hiring an attorney in Chapter 5.

The Home Zone

Now that you're just about ready to start pounding the pavement for your first customers, it's time to investigate one last possible barrier to your business: your local zoning ordinances. These regulations can prohibit small businesses like yours from operating in certain areas, including residential neighborhoods. Such ordinances exist to protect people from excessive traffic and noise (as well as to rake in the extra taxes assessed on businesses). But because you won't have clients visiting your home, it's quite likely you can run the business quietly without anyone being the wiser. But if you intend to park a heavy-duty truck in your driveway that says "Ray's Mowing Service" on the doors, you'd better check with your local government office to see if any special permits are required for homebased businesses. It's better to find out upfront, before you go to the expense of printing stationery and obtaining a business telephone line, than to find out later that such businesses are prohibited.

Not every community will have a problem with equipment stored on your property, however. "I park a lot of vehicles in the driveway, so it looks like 'Beverly Hillbillies' around here," says Lowell P., a lawn care

Beware!

Local governments (cities, townships, and counties) rather than states establish their own zoning regulations, and these regulations vary widely. A homebased business that's perfectly legal in one city could be verboten in another. The only way to find out is by calling the zoning board in your community.

service owner in Stanwood, Washington. "But we live in a remote area on the south end of an island, so no one has said anything...yet."

Other Licenses and Permits

But wait, there's more! Some municipalities require the business owner to have a business license. It's usually available for a very nominal fee and is renewable annually. If, by chance, you're turned down for a license because of zoning restrictions, you can apply for (and probably receive) a variance from the municipal planning commission so you can get your license.

If you're planning to use pesticides and other chemicals in your business, special licensing, as well as certification is usually required. Requirements vary by state. Check with your state agriculture department for specifics on educational requirements, testing, and certification.

Sometimes, you're also required by your state to have other special permits or licenses. For guidance, you can contact:

- *The Small Business Administration (SBA)*. See the federal listings in your phone book, or go to www.sba.gov.
- *Small Business Development Centers*. You can reach these through the SBA, or by logging onto www.sba.gov/SBDC for a list of local offices.
- *Service Corps of Retired Executives*. Go to www.score.org. This nonprofit organization is an SBA partner and has hundreds of chapters throughout the United States.

The Business Plan: Your Navigational Chart

There's one more task you have to complete before you can leave this chapter and plunge into the other uncharted waters that await you. And this is one that literally can make or break your business. You have to write a well-thought-out, persuasive, and comprehensive business plan that will guide you though your business.

Your business plan is like a roadmap. It outlines your plans, goals, and strategies for making your business successful. It's useful not just for applying for credit or attracting investors, but it also gives you direction so you can achieve even your loftiest goals as well as measure the success of your business over time.

Chris B. had an even better reason for writing a business plan. "Without a good business plan, no one will support you and give you the capital you need," he says. "You have to have all your ducks in a row before trying to get financing." There are seven major components a business plan should have. Here's how they apply to a lawn care service business:

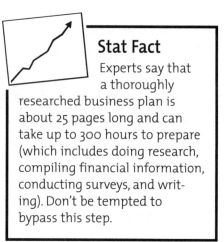

Stat Fact
Experts say that a thoroughly researched business plan is about 25 pages long and can take up to 300 hours to prepare (which includes doing research, compiling financial information, conducting surveys, and writing). Don't be tempted to bypass this step.

- *Executive summary.* In this section, which summarizes the entire business plan, you'll want to describe the nature of your business, the scope of the services you offer (mowing, fertilizing, pest control, irrigation, etc.), the legal form of operation (discussed earlier in this chapter), and your goals. If you expect to use the business plan to seek financing for your company, you should include details about your overall plans, too.

- *Business description.* In the business description section, you'll describe both the lawn care industry and your target market. You'll find general statistics about the industry in Chapter 1 of the book you're holding. But for even more information that can prove helpful in establishing the viability of your business, check the Small Business Development Center Web site at www.sba. gov/SBDC.

- *Market strategies.* Here's another place where all that market research data you've collected will come in handy. In this section, discuss exactly what you'll do to reach customers and how you'll pull it off. Focus, too, on the things that make your company unique, like your knowledge of feng shui in landscaping. You'll find more information about marketing plans in Chapter 9.

- *Competitive analysis.* If you've done your homework well, you already know how many lawn care businesses currently are operating in your target market. But in this section, you should also note other potential competitors, such as snow removal companies that do lawn care during the off-season, lawn and garden stores that have maintenance services, or even homeowners who choose to tend their own lawns. Analyze their strengths and weaknesses, and contrast them against what you consider to be your own strengths.

- *Design and development plan.* Here's where you'll consider how you'll develop market opportunities to help your company prosper and grow. It's helpful to create a timetable of objectives that you can look back on to benchmark your successes, like setting a goal for graduating from servicing 20 customers a week

Start-Up Checklist

❏ Select a business name with the help of the form on pages 39 and 40.

❏ Apply for a dba.

❏ Decide on the best legal form for your business.

❏ Check local zoning regulations to make sure your business will be in compliance.

❏ Apply for a variance if zoning regulations prohibit you from running a home-based business.

❏ Apply for a business license if required in your community.

❏ Write your business plan.

❏ Contact an accountant to discuss the financial and tax requirements related to establishing and operating a business.

to 40, or widening your service area to include a second community. You should also consider how much full- or part-time help you'll need to accomplish these lofty goals.

- *Operations and management plan.* You can use the information in Chapter 2 of this manual as a guide for this section, which discusses the day-to-day operations of your business. You should also create a simple organizational chart—unless, of course, you're the only one on it; then it's not necessary. You also need to include a list of your overhead expenses, which include all the nonlabor expenses you'll accrue, including office expenses like utility bills and office supplies, and business expenses like gasoline for your truck, mower blade sharpening, and supplies like trash bags and fertilizer. You should keep this section updated to reflect any new or expanded services you offer.

- *Financial factors.* Even if you're a sole proprietor with very modest first-year expectations, you need to forecast the success of your business. This will help keep your business on track and help you avoid nasty surprises. Probably the

Tip...

Smart Tip

The SBA offers a number of publications that can guide you through the development of your business plan, including publication MP 21, *Developing a Strategic Business Plan*, and publication MP 15, *Business Plan for Homebased Business*. They're available free at local SBA offices, or by visiting www.sba.gov/library.

most important document in this section should be your balance sheet, which will provide a running tally of how well the business is doing. You'll also need an operating income/expense statement, which is something we'll talk about in Chapter 12.

Constructing such a detailed business plan probably sounds like a lot of useless, boring work. After all, all you really need to do your job is a truck, a lawn mower, and a dry day, as well as some space in your den or on your dining room table for doing paperwork. But embarking on a new business without a clear-cut plan is like sailing for Europe without a navigational chart or a compass. Without a plan, you won't have any idea to whom you're selling your services to or what they're even interested in. So take the time to formalize your business plan now, and refer back to it periodically for both inspiration and direction. You also should revise your plan periodically. For example, if you're not earning as much as you'd hoped, you might need to adjust your prices or delay equipment purchases. Adjust your business plan to reflect changes like these.

The Name Game

Establishing a unique business identity is not just important; it's absolutely essential so prospective clients (and, alas, the IRS) can find you easily. Although it's quite common for lawn service owners to use their own names in their company monikers, that's not your only choice. Try completing the following brainstorming exercise to explore other possible name choices that can either stand alone or be combined with your own name.

List the top three things that come to mind when you hear the word "grass" (such as adjectives like "perfect" or "manicured," or nouns like "carpet"). Be creative!

1. _Green_
2. _Turf_
3. _____

List three unique landmarks or features that characterize the place where you'll do business (such as the abundant lakes in Michigan or the starkly beautiful Black Hills of South Dakota). CAUTION: Avoid weather references like snow belt or desert that will seem incongruous when combined with a lawn care reference!

1. _Bay_
2. _Palm_
3. _____

List three geographical references (such as your city, state, or regional area).

1. _Bay_
2. _Tampa_
3. _Florida_

Now, try combining elements from these three sections in different ways:

1. _Palm Bay Turf_
2. _____
3. _____

Did you come up with something you liked? If not, try using alliteration or plays on words with any of the elements above to create an interesting business name.

The Name Game, continued

Once you've selected a name, put it to the test:

❏ Say it aloud several times to make sure it's easily understood, both in person and over the phone. (Remember the name "Steady Stu's Lawn Service"? It has too many "s" sounds, making it too difficult to pronounce, let alone understand on the phone.)

❏ Thumb through your local Yellow Pages directory to make sure someone else isn't already using the name you've chosen.

❏ Check with your county seat or other official registrar to make sure the name is available (since someone may have already claimed the name but may not be using it yet).

Does your name pass the test? Alrighty then! Now you're ready to register it.

Cutting-Edge
Help

Just as a busy homeowner is happy to turn over the manicuring of his or her property to you, you'll want to relinquish some of the details of running your business to other professionals who have the expertise to do the job right. After all, even if you have the know-how to do your own taxes or review a real estate lease, this isn't necessarily a good use

Photo ©PhotoDisc Inc.

of your time. It's almost always better to spend the lion's share of your working hours on the activity you do best—lawn care—and rely on other professionals to keep your business humming along behind the scenes.

This chapter will give you insight into why you should consider hiring an attorney, an accountant, and an insurance agent, as well as discuss what you can expect them to do for you.

Your Legal Eagle

You're reliable and prompt, conscientious and professional. So you couldn't possibly ever have to worry about being sued by one of your friendly, long-standing clients, right?

A Match Made in Heaven?

Just as every lawn care business owner is different in terms of his or her personal style, temperament, and experience, attorneys are different from one another. The trick is to find a lawyer who meets your personal needs and expectations, and whose strong communication skills make him or her easy to talk to. Here are some general questions to ask that can be helpful in determining whether your attorney-to-be is one you want to have and to hold:

- ○ What is your background and experience?
- ○ What's your specialty?
- ○ How long have you been practicing?
- ○ Do you have other small-business owners as clients?
- ○ Have you ever represented a lawn care service owner before?
- ○ Will you do most of the work, or will a paralegal or other aide help out?
- ○ Is there a charge for the initial consultation?
- ○ What do you charge for routine legal work?
- ○ Do you work on a contingency basis?

Wrong.

Unfortunately, whenever a job involves working with the public, the potential to be sued exists. The lawsuit could be over a matter that you couldn't possibly have controlled, like lightning striking the lawn mower you left under the cover of a weeping willow during a thunderstorm, which caused an electric jolt to travel up the trunk and split it in two. Or you could even be sued by one of your own employees who is hurt on the job.

So it makes sense to retain an attorney *before* anything ever goes wrong so you have someone to turn to for advice and guidance if and when the time comes.

Some of the reasons a lawn care professional might hire an attorney include:

- You want to form a partnership or a corporation
- You find the language in a contract difficult to understand
- You're signing a contract for a lot of money or one that will cover a long period of time, such as an expensive equipment purchase or a long-term lease on an office site
- You're being sued or someone is threatening to sue you

- You need help with tax planning, loan negotiations, employee contracts, and other matters

"But above all, protecting yourself from liability is one of the most important things you must do as a small-business owner," says Daniel H. Minkus, the Michigan attorney. "An attorney can help you assess your risk for being party to a lawsuit and help you minimize it."

As you know from Chapter 4, establishing an LLC or a corporation is a good way to limit the liability on your personal property. Limiting your *financial* liability when hiring an attorney is just as important, especially when you're just starting out and your cash flow is modest.

Minkus says that because you don't need a *litigator* to handle the routine legal work, you can keep the cost down by hiring an attorney in a one- or two-person practice. Attorneys' hourly rates typically run from $100 to $450, with the higher rates being charged by senior partners and those who work at larger firms. Other factors that influence cost include geographic location, the experience of the attorney, and his or her area of expertise.

Because some attorneys charge an initial consultation fee, be sure to ask about it before you ever set foot in his or her office. In addition, you may have to pay your attorney a *retainer* upfront, which he or she will draw against as work is completed. Others charge a *contingency fee*, which means they take a percentage of any lawsuit settlement that's reached. Still others charge a flat fee for routine work, such as filing incorporation papers.

Dollar Stretcher

You may be able to save money on attorneys' fees by joining a prepaid legal plan. After paying a small annual fee, you can get services like telephone consultations, letter writing, and contract review by a qualified attorney. The plan may also provide legal representation at a reduced cost. Not all states sanction these plans. But if yours does, you can find legal networks in the phone directory.

Another way to keep your legal costs reasonable is simply by being organized. "Do your own legwork to gather the information you need beforehand, and limit the number of office visits you make," Minkus advises. "You also should limit phone calls to your attorney, because you'll be charged for those, too."

Many attorneys offer start-up packages that can be affordable for small-business owners. While you can often tailor such packages to meet your needs, they typically include an initial consultation, as well as all activities related to the LLC or incorporation process, including the filing of paperwork with your state and other corporate formalities. You can expect to pay approximately

$500 if you're establishing an LLC, or about $900 if you're setting up a corporation. A payment plan may be available to help you handle the cost.

Locating an attorney you like and respect is often as simple as asking friends or relatives for a referral. In any event, Minkus says getting a referral is much more reliable than just opening the Yellow Pages and picking someone at random. Another way to find a lawyer is through attorney referral services, which are located in many counties throughout the United States. You also could call the American Bar Association at (312) 988-5522, or visit www.findanattorney.com or www.martindale.com.

Money Managers

It's usually easier to convince a new business owner that he or she needs an accountant than to convince them that they need an attorney. Most people either are admirably adept or totally clueless when it comes to budgeting, bookkeeping, and other financial matters. But even those who feel comfortable cranking out their personal taxes annually or investing online may blanche at the thought of creating profit and loss statements and other complex documents. That's usually a pretty reliable sign that you need to book the services of a professional accountant.

An accountant can help you establish an effective record-keeping system, help you keep expenses in line, and monitor cash flow. He or she also can advise you on tax issues, which is crucial because tax law is very complicated and changes frequently. (The IRS issues new tax rulings every two hours of every business day!) Tax issues that might be relevant to a lawn care professional include the amount you can deduct annually for business expenses (including travel and office equipment) and the amount of money you can deposit to your retirement account annually.

Like an attorney, an accountant experienced in handling small-business tax issues also can advise you whether you should incorporate your business. In addition to protecting your personal assets, incorporating can cut your tax bill, allow you to put more money into your personal investments, and offer other useful benefits.

There are two types of accountants. Certified public accountants, or CPAs, are college-educated and have to pass a rigorous certification examination in the state where

> **Tip...**
>
> **Smart Tip**
>
> Hiring an enrolled agent instead of an accountant can save you money if you're only looking for tax help. In addition to preparing your tax return, enrolled agents can represent you before the IRS. They can be found in the Yellow Pages or through the National Association of Enrolled Agents (www.naea.org).

they do business in order to put those coveted letters after their names. Public accountants aren't certified and don't have to be licensed by the state. While they may be perfectly capable due to their experience, they usually can't represent you before the IRS if you're called in for an audit.

There's also a wide range of accounting software on the market that can help you crunch the numbers and manage your business accounting. QuickBooks is the choice of many lawn care business owners. Keep in mind, however, that some of the other packages around may not satisfy IRS requirements for record-keeping. It's probably wiser to rely on a professional to handle accounting matters whenever you need to do anything more complex than record credits and debits or informally tally up business expenditures.

To find an accountant, ask your attorney, banker, or other business professionals you deal with for a referral. The American Institute of Certified Public Accountants' branch in your state also can refer you to a qualified number-cruncher, or you can refer to its Web site at www.aicpa.org. It's very important to select someone who has experience either with small-business clients in general, or lawn care business owners in particular (although, this can be a pretty tall order). Avoid accountants who specialize in large corporations, since they're not likely to be as familiar with small-business concerns as you'd like.

Accountants charge $75 to $125 an hour and up. You can keep your accountant's costs down by organizing your financial records and receipts before you meet (overflowing shoeboxes are not considered a viable accounting system!). You'll find more bookkeeping strategies and advice in Chapter 12.

Covering Your Assets

The other business professional you should have on your side is an insurance agent. Although you could use one of those online services that guide you to discount insurance brokers, it's usually better (and less time-consuming) to find an agent in your own community instead (or at least at the time of start-up; you can comparison shop and switch later). This will allow you to discuss the particulars of your own business with an agent to make sure you're covered against all potential pitfalls. Face-to-face interaction is the best way to accomplish this. It's also the most reliable way for you to get adequate coverage. An experienced agent will be familiar with the risks you might encounter in your business and can recommend exactly how much coverage you need to protect yourself against those risks.

The easiest way to locate an insurance agent who can help you with your business needs is by contacting the person who currently insures your home, apartment, or automobile. Alternately, you can find agents listed in the phone book under "Insurance."

Types of Insurance

Figuring out which kind of business insurance you need can be a dizzying proposition. Insurance is necessary for risk management because it's so easy to sustain a loss that could force you into bankruptcy. The trouble is, you can also go bankrupt trying to protect yourself against every possible situation that could result in litigious action. So in this section, we'll discuss some of the types of insurance you may need for your lawn care business and let you decide for yourself which ones to spring for. Don't have a clue where to start? One reasonable way to approach the process is to decide how much of a loss you could personally afford to cover and buy insurance to offset the rest of the risk.

If you don't have an insurance agent, now's the time to find one, since he or she can help you muddle through this somewhat confusing—and expensive—process. We also recommend looking for package insurance deals and obtaining cost estimates from at least two reliable agents since prices can vary so widely.

Basically, you need two kinds of insurance: insurance to cover the loss of or damage to your equipment, as well as injuries to employees, and insurance to cover damage to clients' lawns or property due to errors or negligence.

Here are the types of insurance that will cover these two situations:

- *Commercial general liability (CGL).* Every lawn care business owner we spoke with has this type of insurance. It covers any kind of bodily injury, including injuries caused by employees operating a company vehicle, as well as property damage or loss, like if your lawn mower throws a rock through a customer's bay window. It also covers personal injury as a result of slander or damage to one's reputation, although this is not a common occurrence in the lawn care industry (unless you unfairly impugn another lawn care professional's reputation and he decides to sue). You'll still need to supplement your CGL insurance with workers' compensation and auto insurance, but this policy is pretty comprehensive. In fact, most of the other types of insurance mentioned below are included in the standard CGL policy. You can expect to pay $300 to $800 a year for $500,000 to $1 million worth of coverage, according to Michelle Parker, an independent insurance agent in New Baltimore, Michigan.

- *Fire and general property insurance.* This covers fire losses, vandalism, and weather-related damage, but it's only necessary if you own or rent a commercial building. Homebased businesses would purchase a business owner's policy instead (see "business owner's policy" on next page).

- *Fidelity bonding.* This is "honesty" insurance, so to speak, that protects businesses and their clients from financial losses due to dishonest employees. Parker says it's unusual for lawn care or landscaping businesses to be bonded, but some people consider it a sign of trustworthiness on the part of the business owner. (Just check the Yellow Pages under services like plumbing to see how often the word "bonded" pops up.) You have to pay for bonding for every job you do, which will cost about $50 per job for a year's coverage. That means if you have 15 customers and you wish to be bonded for all of them, it will cost you $750.

> ## Smart Tip
> Tip...
>
> There's a difference between insurance agents and brokers. Insurance agents usually represent one company. Insurance brokers, on the other hand, are independent professionals who represent you and can recommend the policies of many different companies. You may be able to save a significant amount of money working with a broker. Check your state's insurance department for a list of reputable brokers.

- *Business-interruption.* This replaces business income and pays for expenses like equipment, office rent, etc., after a fire, theft, or other insured loss. This isn't a common stand-alone policy for lawn service owners.

- *Business owner's policy (BOP).* This is a comprehensive package that provides general liability ($500,000 limit), fraud insurance, and business-interruption insurance for homebased businesses. This multi-insurance package is usually more affordable than buying separate policies and is an alternative to purchasing the CGL policy, which only covers personal injury and property damage. It costs an average of $250 to $350 per year. Consider your insurance options carefully and choose the policies that best fit your needs.

- *Business auto.* This is just the thing you need to cover your company truck. The costs vary widely depending on the number of vehicles you have, the type and size of the vehicle, where the vehicle is parked, the radius it's driven from home base, and the cargo it carries.

- *Workers' compensation.* This compensates employees for work-related injuries, diseases, and illnesses. Most states require employers to carry this type of insurance, and the cost varies by state. In Michigan, for instance, the cost is $6 for every $100 of employee payroll since lawn care is considered a fairly low-risk business. If you're lucky, you may be in a state that doesn't require workers' comp if you only have one employee (and by the way, you personally don't count as an employee). But even if you don't need workers' comp, you do need insurance against work-related injury lawsuits. Talk to an insurance agent for advice.

Use this business insurance planning worksheet to take notes on the different types of insurance you may need.

Business Insurance Planning Worksheet

Type	Required	Annual Cost
Payment schedule		
Commercial general liability		
Fire and general property		
Fidelity bonding		
Business-interruption		
Business owner's policy		
Business auto		
Workers' compensation		
Total Annual Cost		

Tools
of the Trade

Now that you've got all that pesky administrative stuff out of the way, it's time to start thinking about the fun stuff—namely, the toys you'll need to run this grand enterprise of yours. If you've always had a love of and knack for caring for your own lawn, you may already have enough maintenance equipment to get your business off the ground.

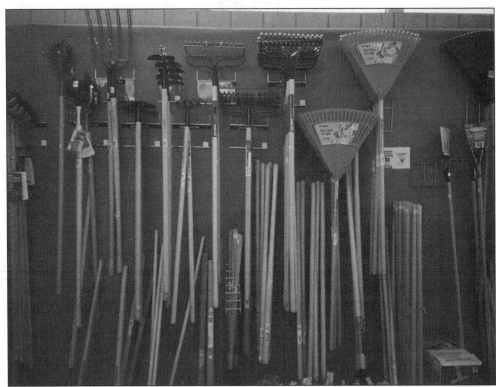

Photo ©PhotoDisc Inc.

Of course, it's always more fun to go shopping for newer, bigger, more powerful equipment. After all, this is a serious business you'll be running, and serious businesses need serious tools. Plus, you may discover that the mower and other equipment you have parked in your tool shed may not be powerful enough for the daily punishment you're going to give it. So this chapter will discuss the various tools you'll need to run the business and will help you take a systematic approach to estimating your start-up costs so you know whether you need to seek outside financing.

Lawn Maintenance Equipment

The basics you need to get your business off the ground fall into roughly four categories: lawn maintenance equipment, office equipment (including furniture and business machines like computers), office supplies, and business services. You'll find a worksheet on pages 67 and 68 that you can use to estimate and calculate your total start-up costs in each of these four categories. And check out pages 64 through 66, where we provide start-up expenses for two hypothetical lawn care businesses.

52

Toys of the Trade

If you decide to offer landscaping as part of your service mix, here's a list of the basic tools you'll need to work on gardens, berms, flower beds, and other landscaped areas:

- Pointed and square-edged shovels (for turning loose earth)
- Spade (for digging just about anything else)
- Spading fork (square-tined, which won't bend out of shape)
- Hoes (long-handled for cultivating; scuffle hoe for cutting weeds)
- Pick (for piercing)
- Mattock (for cutting and chopping roots)
- Hoses (50-footers are standard, with a 1-inch diameter and cast solid-brass connectors)
- Dandelion tool (a chisel-like tool that can fit in your back pocket)
- Pruners (with a sheath)
- Loppers (for chopping off heavy branches)
- Pruning saw (for getting in between branches)
- Hedge shears (the low-tech manual type for shaping topiaries, electric or gas shears for hedges)
- Leather gloves (because gripping these tools can be murder on your hands, and because spiny weeds can cut right through regular garden gloves)

You'll also want to wear long sleeves and goggles to protect yourself from flying debris while you're working. Work boots are also a must.

Truck

Your biggest expenditure by far will be for the purchase of a sturdy, reliable vehicle for hauling your equipment if you don't already own a truck that can serve this purpose. A ¾-ton pickup truck or utility van with a trailer hitch will fill the bill if you're concentrating on servicing residential and small commercial customers. A basic truck costs around $25,000 new. If you're going to be doing a lot of commercial work, opt for a larger 1½-ton pickup, which will cost $30,000 or more.

But you don't have to sink a lot of dough in a factory-fresh model. A used vehicle is often a better value because you'll save a lot on the purchase price and pay less in insurance premiums, to boot. And generally speaking, it's better to purchase than lease

> **Beware!**
>
> Don't spend too much money on the vehicle you'll use to transport yourself and your equipment to job sites. Although comfort and maybe a few cup holders are important, you won't be spending that much time in the truck or van to warrant expensive options like a CD player, a sunroof, or fancy detailing.

your vehicle. You'll be loading and unloading heavy equipment that will be covered with oil, grass clippings, and dirt, resulting in significant wear and tear on the vehicle. You can avoid the stiff penalties the leasing companies assess for excessive wear and tear when you buy instead. Chances are, it won't cost you much more to buy a used truck than it would to lease a new one.

After you've settled on a truck, make a beeline for the nearest sign shop and order a magnetic sign or decal with your company name and phone number. You can have custom signs made up for about $60. (See "Magnetic Signs" in the Appendix for the names of businesses you can contact on the Internet.) Decals cost even less but won't last as long.

Once you have your signs, be sure to park your truck in a prominent place in front of your job sites to garner free publicity while you work.

Utility Trailer

This is a must if you have a lot of equipment and you don't want to be hoisting it up repeatedly into your van or your truck bed. These plain-Jane conveyances consist of a flat bed, one axle, and metal rails. A 5-by-10-foot model with a ramp gate (also a must so you can wheel mowers aboard) will run about $800 new. Check your local classified ads for a less expensive used model.

Lowell P. in Stanwood, Washington, swears by the used boat trailer he bought for $150—with a boat still on it. "We had a nice bonfire in the front yard when we brought it home," he says, laughing.

Last but not least, invest in locking tie-downs to keep your equipment safe when you're on the road. A package of four 6-foot tie-downs will run about $11.

Vehicle Alarm System

With all that expensive equipment you'll be hauling around to job sites, you might want to consider installing an alarm system on your vehicle. By far the most economical system is the alarm/kill switch combination. Any more than that probably isn't necessary, because perpetrators are probably more likely to try to swipe the whole rig rather than breaking in to steal individual tools or machines. Some vehicles come equipped with this feature, but if yours doesn't, it will cost you $50 to $100 to have a system professionally installed.

Storage Facility

Just as you can work out of a home office, you can start your business without the overhead cost of a storage facility by using your own garage. In addition to sheltering your vehicle, you'll want to use the space to do repairs and store equipment and extra supplies like trash bags and fertilizer. You can pick up heavy-duty industrial shelving for about $69 and standard utility shelving for about $25 at a home improvement store. But if you don't have enough room in your garage or carport, you'll have to find another facility because many cities have ordinances that prohibit parking commercial vehicles on residential streets overnight. An alternative to your garage would be to rent a bay in a self-storage facility. A space as small as 10-by-15 feet, which is about the size of a large bedroom, is sufficient for lawn equipment and miscellaneous supplies. If you want to park your truck inside, you'll need about 10-by-20 feet (a small one-car garage size), or 10-by-30 feet if you want to pull your trailer in, too. The rent varies widely according to which part of the country you live in, but you can expect to pay $100 to $200 a month.

Uniforms and Hats

Although not technically equipment like your truck or mower, apparel that bears your company name and logo can be just as important to your business. Personalized T-shirts and hats not only give you a neat, professional appearance, but they also function as low-cost advertising tools. And here's an added bonus: The IRS actually considers shirts that have your company name and logo on them to be advertising and will allow you to deduct their cost. Other work clothes, including work pants or jeans and steel-toed shoes, are not deductible.

Embroidered polo shirts cost around $28 each, T-shirts cost around $13 each, and hats run about $12 to $17 each.

Lawn Mowers

There's a dizzying array of lawn mowers on the market. These days, most are self-propelled, a feature you'll greatly appreciate after you've spent hours crisscrossing acres of green grass under the blazing sun. Mowers often come with very useful attachments and features like mulchers and side catchers that can make your job easier. For bigger jobs, a riding mower is a necessity, but for the purposes of this book, we'll assume you'll be using a standard walk-behind model.

Since you're planning to make a go of lawn care as a business, invest in a good commercial mower rather than just using the one in your garage. Properly maintained, a commercial model can mow many lawns for years to come with minimal engine trouble. In contrast, the mowers you buy from your local discount or department

▲

store might only last for a single season, depending on how many lawns you mow. What you can do, however, is keep your nonprofessional mower as a backup if your primary mower needs servicing.

Commercial walk-behind lawn mowers come in widths from 21 to 60 inches. You can get a reliable mower for $799 to $2,799. Of course, you can spend even more if you want. For instance, a top-of-the-line Husqvarna riding mower, which has a top ground speed of 10 mph, can cost $6,995! Like your truck or car, you usually can negotiate the price down when you buy from a dealer who specializes in lawn care equipment. Some well-known commercial equipment manufacturers include Exmark, John Deere, and Scag.

The warranties on commercial mowers (and other equipment, for that matter) tend to be very short—as short as 90 days—because of the rough treatment they get. For the same reason, it's usually not possible to buy an extended warranty. But some lawn equipment dealers do offer zero-downtime coverage at an extra cost so you have the use of a comparable loaner while your machine is in the shop. This type of policy costs a few hundred dollars a year and might be worth it if you're the cautious type.

If you work with a partner or an employee, or if you send a crew out to a job site, a second commercial mower is a must. That way, when the person who's doing the edging, trimming, and other work finishes up first, he or she can wheel out the second mower to assist the main mower.

Finally, before you can mow, you need to know exactly how much lawn you're working with so you can give an estimate to a prospect. A measuring wheel runs about $25.

Safety Equipment

Anyone who works with power equipment should consider wearing ear protection. Lawn equipment operates at up to 95 decibels, and according to OSHA, hearing damage can occur with even limited exposure to sound levels in the 85-to-90-dk range. Ear protectors that look like stereo headphones are affordably priced at around $14 a pair.

While you're at it, invest in a sturdy pair of safety glasses. They're not very stylish, but they'll protect your eyes from rocks and other projectiles churned up by your mower or other equipment. They're a bargain at about $8 a pair.

You should also wear work gloves while on the job. They give you a firmer grip on the handles of your equipment, which is especially important when your hands are sweating in hot weather. Opt for inexpensive gloves—as long as they're reasonably durable—since they're so easily misplaced or lost. Gloves usually cost only a few dollars.

Steel-toed work boots are another important part of your workday ensemble. At an average of $90 a pair, they're on the steep side, but they can save you a world of hurt and prevent costly medical bills. Buy the best you can afford (they can cost upwards of $200), and make sure they have good arch support.

The final thing you should stock up on is sunblock. You're going to be in full or hazy sunlight every day you're on the job, and studies have shown that prolonged exposure to the sun (particularly during the peak hours of 10 A.M. to 3 P.M.) increases your risk of developing skin cancer, including deadly melanoma. No matter the color of your skin, you need a sunscreen with a minimum of SPF 15 to protect your skin. And don't forget to wear a visored hat (with your company logo, of course) to shield both your face and your scalp even after you've applied sunscreen.

Spreaders and Sprayers

Even if your intent is to stick to mowing, it's a good idea to offer fertilizing as one of your basic services. For that, you'll need a broadcast granular spreader, which, as the name implies, disperses the fertilizer in a wide arc. Spreaders cost around $35.

To attack weeds growing in cracks in the sidewalk or driveway, invest in a small, two-gallon pressurized herbicide sprayer. It will run about $30.

The Final Four

You'll need four more pieces of commercial equipment to groom your customers' lawns to perfection: a trimmer, edger, blower, and hedge trimmer. The trimmer is used to reach grass that grows in places the mower can't reach, like around trees or mailbox posts. A commercial model will run $200 to $400. An edger removes the grass that grows over the edge of driveways, sidewalks, and other borders, and a commercial version will cost $250 to $450. A backpack blower is used to direct stray clippings back onto the lawn, and can cost $300 to $600, although a commercial-quality blower may not be necessary. However, you will want to opt for one with the most powerful motor to help you get the job done faster. Finally, a hedge trimmer puts the finishing touches on those stately borders. An electric model will cost around $250 to $350, but can be a pain because you have to hunt around for an outside electrical outlet. Lawn service people often prefer just to use a low-tech manual trimmer ($10) instead.

Some lawn care equipment manufacturers offer machines that are edgers and trimmers combined. Redmax makes a split-boom (shaft) multihead tool that retails for $399 that can be fitted with a $100 edger attachment. While these combination tools will save you a few bucks and some space in the garage or shed, they're not recommended for people who groom lawns for a living unless they have a very small client base—say ten customers or fewer.

With all the equipment you'll need, now you can see why you need a truck to operate this business!

Office Equipment

Yes, the primary equipment you'll be using in your daily business is lawn care equipment, but don't think you can start this business with a lawn mower and edger alone. You'll need plenty of office equipment to keep the administrative side of your business in tip-top shape. Here, we discuss all the office equipment you may need.

Furniture

Since you'll be doing most of your work out in the wide open spaces, you may not think it's necessary to establish a specific work space at home. After all, you can stuff invoices at the dining room table while grabbing a late-night sandwich or set up your laptop on the patio when you want to do your scheduling for the month, right?

Well, yes. But even though you can run your business from whatever corner of the house is relatively free of video games and laundry, you'll be much more productive and feel much more professional if you set up a permanent office space somewhere in the house, even if it's just in a secluded corner. This is especially important if you have children around who are always clamoring for a game of catch, a ride to the park, or assistance dressing Barbie. You just need to teach them that when Daddy is in his "work space," he can't be interrupted. This goes for Mommy as well.

The basic requirements for your work space are an inexpensive desk or computer workstation, a comfortable office chair (preferably one that's ergonomic, since you'll

Dollar Stretcher

A sheet of sanded and stained plywood laid on top of a pair of two-drawer file cabinets makes a sturdy and inexpensive desk. The desk will be exactly the right height and will provide plenty of storage and work space.

be spending a lot of time in it), and a sturdy two- or four-drawer file cabinet. You should also consider acquiring a bookcase so you can keep your reference materials conveniently at hand.

Office supply stores like Staples and Office Depot sell reasonably priced office furniture that will set you back only about $200 to $600 for a desk, and $60 to $250 for a chair. In addition, you often can save a substantial amount of money on your desk or computer workstation by purchasing furniture that must be assembled (known as KD or "knock down") or by scouring the classified ads for used furniture. A two-drawer letter-sized file cabinet costs $25 to $100, while a four-shelf bookcase will cost around $70.

Personal Computers

You can't escape them: PCs are now a way of life. They offer speed, convenience, and compatibility with other users. They use sophisticated yet user-friendly software packages to crunch numbers, churn out billing statements, figure your taxes, and connect you to the Internet. Best of all, this efficiency and accuracy is now available at a cost that's reasonable, even for a fledgling small-business owner—usually around $1,200 to $3,000 for a complete Pentium-based system that includes the hard drive, monitor, mouse, modem, and printer.

Albert T. Detroit, chose to build his own computer—a powerful 900MHz monster with 320MB RAM that blazes through every task he undertakes. "Building it myself was the only way I could get the power I wanted," he says. "Between the business and the B.S. degree in turfgrass management I'm working on, I needed the speed."

Since the most common business software packages take a lot of memory, your system should have at least a 10GB hard drive, 64MB RAM, and a processor speed of 433MHz. It should come equipped with no less than a 24X CD-ROM so you can load most software packages, as well as internal fax and modem cards.

Other useful adds-ons that are nice to have but are not essential for lawn care owners include: a scanner (which range from $150 to $300, depending on the resolution); a CD-RW (or CD rewritable) drive, which allows you to download data onto CDs ($300 to $400); a Zip drive ($100 to $200) for long-term data storage of records and photo files if you do landscaping; and a digital camera ($200 to $500), which allows you to download landscaping photographs directly to your computer.

Dollar Stretcher

If you're on a tight budget, you can save a lot of money on your computer by buying used equipment. As long as the CPU isn't ancient (meaning more than a year old), you can upgrade the memory and bring it up to speed for considerably less than buying new.

▲

Software

Most of the lawn care business owners we spoke with use two basic software packages for conducting business: Microsoft Office and QuickBooks. Microsoft Office is a bundled package that includes word processing, spreadsheet, database management, e-mail, presentation, and scheduling programs and retails for about $600. QuickBooks is an easy-to-use accounting package that not only keeps your financial records, but also can manage your business checking account and print checks. The Pro version retails for about $250.

There are also a few lawn care business software packages worth mentioning. The owners we spoke with favored CLIP from Sensible Software Inc. Four different packages are available, with prices ranging from $200 to $5,000. Among the features they offer are scheduling, routing, and job-costing. You also can transfer billing information directly to QuickBooks to generate invoices.

Other green-industry-specific software worth checking out includes Real Green, which can track 8,000 lawn care accounts and includes a mapping function for daily routing (call for price); Route Rite ($1,195), which includes customer history, routing and scheduling, and accounts receivable modules; Lawn Monkey ($379, or $183 for a one-year lease), with geographical zone and date-based scheduling capabilities; and GroundsKeeper Pro ($290), business management software for landscapers and lawn service professionals, which offers a free demo download at its Web site at www.adkad.com/groundskeeper/gkpro2000.htm. See the Appendix for information on where to buy these software products.

Telephones and Answering Machines

Bright Idea

To make your outgoing message sound as professional as possible, practice it a few times before recording it. The message should include your business name and a statement about when the caller can expect a return call. Don't play music or—horrors!—have lawn mower sound effects in the background. This is a lawn care business, not a recording studio.

A phone is an essential piece of equipment, and you should buy the best one you can afford. A standard two-line speakerphone with auto redial, memory dial, flashing lights, mute button, and other useful features will run $70 to $150, while a top-of-the-line model can cost $250 or more. A great source for high-quality phones is Hello Direct (see Appendix), which carries the Polycom line of professional business telephones. And while you're at it, consider purchasing a phone with a headset for hands-free calling so you can prevent the discomfort caused by cradling the receiver between your neck and shoulder.

Your answering machine is another must-have for the times when you're away from the office or you're trying to do some paperwork without interruption. Many answering machines come as part of a cordless phone unit and have plenty of cool bells and whistles. One of the most useful features allows you to call in from a remote location and pick up your messages, which you'll appreciate when you're actively seeking new clients. A stand-alone answering machine may cost $40 to $150, while a cordless phone/answering machine combo will run $50 to nearly $200.

Cellular phones have also become a necessity for lawn care professionals, who use them to keep in touch with employees, call customers, and return calls while en route to job sites. If you play your cards right, you'll receive a brand-new phone at no charge at the time of service activation. Otherwise, you can expect to pay up to $200 for a reliable phone. See the "Business Services" section on pages 62 and 63 for a rundown of monthly service charges.

Copy Machines

No one says you have to have a copy machine right in your office, especially when quickie print shops like Kinko's and Sir Speedy Printing are so conveniently located around the country. But you can't beat the convenience of having your own copier nearby, especially now that they cost as little as $500 to $1,000 for a standard business machine. They use toner cartridges that are readily available from your local office supply store and sell for $10 to $15.

A really small or part-time lawn care business probably can do without its own copier. But if you want one, check your local Yellow Pages directory for the names and numbers of dealers in your area.

Office Supplies

After spending all that money on lawn care equipment, you'll be relieved to know that office supplies will cause barely a ripple in your budget. One of your most important purchases will be a box of professionally printed business cards. They don't have to be fancy. Black lettering on white card stock looks professional and gets the job done. Print shops like Kinko's and office supply stores like Office Depot can whip up cards for you at a reasonable cost (around $30 for 250 business cards). There are also a number of mail order printing companies like Amsterdam Printing & Litho Corp. and New England Business Service Inc. that offer a wide selection of paper, printing styles, and colors to choose from delivery as well as right to your door.

Alternately, if you're operating on a real shoestring budget, you can purchase blank business cards from an office supply store and make your own on your office printer.

Dollar Stretcher

Rummage through your desk drawers before heading to the office supply store. You'll probably find all the pens, paper, and paperclips you need to get started. One thing you'll need that you won't have hidden away in a drawer is a box of business cards.

A pack of 250 printable business cards runs under $7 and can be produced in minutes.

The other thing you're going to need is invoices and No. 10 window envelopes so you can bill your clients on a regular basis. You can get custom-printed invoices from the same sources listed above (500 cost about $70). While you're at it, invest in #10 envelopes with windows and have your company name and address imprinted on the face (500 will cost around $65). Using custom-printed invoices makes your business look professional, stable, and reliable.

Finally, you'll need estimate forms. You can make these up yourself on your printer, since the ones available in office supply stores are too general. You'll find a sample estimate form on page 69.

As far as other office supply costs go, you can enter $150 on the worksheet on page 68, which will buy a lot of pens, pads, copy paper, file folders, and wastebaskets.

Business Services

Now that you have an idea what it will cost to outfit your new business in terms of tangible goods, you also must factor in the cost of the services that are required to actually use some of those products.

Telephone charges are likely to make up the lion's share of the service fees you'll pay on a monthly basis. These charges vary regionally, but it's reasonable to estimate a cost of $25 a month per line. Useful features you'll want to consider adding to your basic service include voice mail ($6 to $20 per month), call waiting (approximately $5 per month), and caller ID (around $7.50 for number identification and $2 for name and number identification).

There are a lot of great cellular phone deals around right now, ranging from $5 a month for a no-minute basic package (minutes are charged separately at a rate of 25 to 45 cents each), to $40 for 600 "free" minutes. Because these high-end packages are so reasonable, you might want to opt for one right

Bright Idea

You can create just about any type of form on your PC when you're in a pinch or you want to save a few bucks. Many software programs, like Microsoft Office, come with templates for invoices, purchase orders, time sheets, and other useful forms that can be adapted to your needs.

You Gotta Spend It to Make It

Just about anything you purchase for use in your business is deductible on your federal income taxes, provided you have the proper written documentation (like receipts and packing slips). The Section 179 expense deduction currently allows you to deduct up to $20,000 a year for equipment costs, including computers, office furniture, telecommunications equipment (phones, answering machines, telephone headsets), and fax machines. Other incidentals needed to run the business like office supplies and professional journals and trade magazines are also deductible. If any of these items are used for both business and pleasure (like if your kids use the PC to research dinosaurs for a school project), you can only deduct the amount of time the computer is actually in service for the business. The IRS recommends keeping a log right next to the computer so you can jot down notes about business vs. personal usage.

Happily, other costs typically incurred by lawn care entrepreneurs, including professional fees for attorneys and CPAs, advertising and marketing costs, business equipment repairs, voice mail, seminars taken to improve business skills, trade show and conference fees, and bank fees, may be written off against the business's taxes.

off the bat, since you'll be locked into a certain rate plan for a predetermined number of years anyway. What's really great is that many of these package plans offer thousands of minutes of calling time free on the weekend, when you'll probably be out mowing anyway. You can expect to pay an activation fee of around $30 if you don't sign up for a three-year contract.

You'll also incur a monthly charge (billed in advance to your credit card) to connect your computer to the Internet. You normally have four service choices. The least expensive service is delivered by an Internet Service Provider (ISP), which charges $20 to $25 per month for unlimited usage and uses the modem that comes with your computer. There are many other, faster, Internet connection options.

Last but not least, you may choose to rent a P.O. box or a box at a mailing center like Mail Boxes Etc. as a way of keeping your business mail separate from your personal mail. This service fee will run around $10 to $20 a month.

If you've been penciling in your estimated costs on the worksheet on pages 67 and 68 as you read this chapter, you can now tally everything up to get a pretty clear idea of how much capital it will take to get your new lawn care business started. Need a little financial help to get the ball rolling? See Chapter 12 for advice about approaching bankers and obtaining financing.

Start-Up Expenses

Here are the start-up expenses for two hypothetical lawn care businesses that provide basic mowing and trimming services. The Yard Man is a homebased company whose owner has an office in the corner of his den. He financed the start-up with his personal credit cards. Mowing Masters is also homebased and has top-of-the-line maintenance and business equipment. The owner employs two part-time workers at a rate of $10 per hour.

The Yard Man, which is a part-time business, has a projected annual gross income of $22,400 a year (20 clients at $40 per week for 28 weeks of the year), while Mowing Masters, which is a full-time business servicing an affluent area, expects to earn $56,000 a year (40 clients at $50 per week for 28 weeks of the year). Each business owner takes a percentage of the net profits as income.

The Yard Man's owner uses a personal truck he already owned for the business, while Mowing Masters' owner purchased a company vehicle outright.

Item	The Yard Man (Low)	Mowing Masters (High)
Lawn Maintenance Equipment		
Vehicle	$0	$17,000
Trailer	250	800
Magnetic signs	60	60
Security system	69	69
Mower	699	1,999
Trimmer	200	400
Edger	250	450
Blower	300	600
Steel rake	8	8
Leaf rake	5	5
Industrial broom	25	25
Manual hedge trimmer	10	10
Machete	5	5
Gas can	8	8
Granular spreader	35	35
Pressurized sprayer	30	30
Measuring wheel	25	25

Start-Up Expenses, continued

Item	The Yard Man (Low)	Mowing Masters (High)
Lawn Maintenance Equipment (cont.)		
Steel-toed boots	$90	$150
Safety glasses	8	16
Hearing protectors	14	28
Work gloves (2 pairs)	8	8
Work shirts (5 per person)	65	280
Hats with company logo (5)	60	60
Steel shelving units	69	138
Tie-down straps	22	22
Office Equipment		
Computer, printer	$2,000	$4,000
General software	850	850
Lawn care software	290	1,200
Copy machine	0	500
Phone	70	150
Answering machine	50	100
Postage meter/scale	0	25
Desk	200	500
Chair	100	200
File cabinet(s)	50	200
Bookcase(s)	100	100
Office Supplies		
Invoices, envelopes, business cards	$165	$165
Miscellaneous supplies	50	75
Business Services		
Employee wages (five months)	$0	$4,800
Advertising	30	100

Start-Up Expenses, continued

Item	The Yard Man (Low)	Mowing Masters (High)
Legal services	$0	$900
Insurance (annual premium)	300	1,150
Workers' comp	$0	$288
Market research	0	500
Business license	35	35
Pesticide applicator's license	0	50
Certification/training	225	225
Membership dues (annual)	285	375
Publications (12-month subscriptions)	30	30
Phone service (6 months)	150	150
Cell phone service (6 months)	240	240
Online service	20	20
Web site design	0	800
Web hosting	0	20
P.O. box (6 months)	0	120
Subtotal	**$7,555**	**$40,099**
Miscellaneous expenses	756	4,010
(add roughly 10% of total)		
Total Start-Up Expenses	**$8,311**	**$44,109**

Start-Up Expenses Worksheet

Item

Lawn Maintenance Equipment

Vehicle $ _____

Trailer _____

Magnetic signs _____

Security system _____

Mower _____

Trimmer _____

Edger _____

Blower _____

Steel rake _____

Leaf rake _____

Industrial broom _____

Manual hedge trimmer _____

Machete _____

Gas can _____

Granular spreader _____

Pressurized sprayer _____

Measuring wheel _____

Steel-toed boots _____

Safety glasses _____

Hearing protectors _____

Work gloves (2 pairs) _____

Work shirts (5 per person) _____

Hats with company logo (5) _____

Steel shelving units _____

Tie-down straps _____

Office Equipment

Computer, printer $_____

General software _____

Lawn software _____

Copy machine _____

Start-Up Expenses Worksheet, continued

Phone   _____

Answering machine   _____

Postage meter/scale   _____

Desk   _____

Chair   _____

File cabinet(s)   _____

Bookcase(s)   _____

Office Supplies

Invoices, envelopes, business cards $_____

Miscellaneous supplies (pens, folders, etc.)   _____

Business Services

Employee wages (five months) $_____

Advertising   _____

Legal services   _____

Insurance (annual premium)   _____

Workers' comp   _____

Market research   _____

Business license   _____

Pesticide applicator's license   _____

Certification/training   _____

Membership dues (annual)   _____

Publications (12-month subscriptions)   _____

Phone service (6 months)   _____

Cell phone service (6 months)   _____

Online service   _____

Web site design   _____

Web hosting   _____

P.O. box (6 months)   _____

Subtotal $_____

Miscellaneous expenses   _____

(add roughly 10% of total)

Total Start-Up Expenses $_____

Estimate Form

MOWING MASTERS

5555 Regal Drive

Kissimmee, Florida 55555

(407) 555-5555

ESTIMATE FOR LAWN SERVICES

Date _____, 200x

Prepared for:

NAME _____

ADDRESS_____

_____

Area to be mowed/treated:

    Front lawn _____   square feet

    Back lawn _____   square feet

    Full lawn _____   square feet

Price for weekly mowing service _____

Price for fertilizer application _____ per treatment

Schedule: Every six weeks from March through September

We also offer aeration, power raking, and reseeding at an additional charge. We would be pleased to quote you a price on these services at your request.

Thank you for the opportunity to provide you with this estimate. We'll call you in the next few days to see whether we can be of service. And remember—your satisfaction is always fully guaranteed with Mowing Masters.

Sincerely,

Dan Williams

Owner

Turf
Tenders

Looking for a way to grow your business, unload some of the burden of its day-to-day operations, or dig your way out of a pile of paperwork? Then hire a few employees.

Lawn service owners usually start out as sole proprietors. But let's say you've established a nice, steady customer base that you can handle easily yourself—say, 20 regulars per week. Then, suddenly, a really tasty piece of business, like the cemetery contract Ken W. has in Michigan, drops into your lap. That particular job will require you to be out mowing vast vistas and trimming between headstones all day long for a couple of weeks each month. You can't neglect your residential customers during that time or they won't be your customers for very long. So hiring an employee—or maybe two— is the answer.

Unfortunately, becoming an employer can be like opening Pandora's box—full of "government red tape." Among the parties that will suddenly become extremely interested in you are the IRS (in addition to the keen personal interest it already has in your affairs), the Social Security Administration, OSHA, your state taxing agency, your state agriculture department (if you handle chemicals), and so on. It's enough to make a grown business owner cry. The trick is to do your crying all the way to the bank. So in this chapter, we'll show you some efficient ways to hire, motivate, and compensate in the pursuit of bigger profits.

Diving Into the Labor Pool

Finding qualified help can be a real challenge. There aren't that many people available these days to fill all the service industry jobs that exist. (Just take a drive around your community and check out all the "Help Wanted" signs in the windows.) And while mowing doesn't necessarily take a great deal of technical skill, it is hard work, and it's work that's often done under uncomfortably warm conditions. It also takes a fair amount of physical stamina and the ability to handle power tools deftly without amputating body parts. So what on earth would make someone take on such a demanding job when he or she could sell designer shoes at the mall or call out mystery game numbers at the bowling alley?

M-O-N-E-Y, that's what. Which is why you'll have to do better than minimum wage if you want to attract qualified workers.

"Don't fall off your chair, but part of my success in hiring employees has come from paying way past the industry standard," says Nathan B. in Sykesville, Maryland. "I pay laborers $11 to $14 an hour and my foreman $17 an hour. That may seem like a lot, but I've kept my employees [a long time]—one has been with me six years, and two others have been around three years. That's pretty much unheard of in this business."

In case you did fall off your chair, remember that the trade-off for shelling out the big bucks is that, like Nathan, you won't have to spend a lot of time advertising, interviewing, and hiring. But you don't necessarily have to pay that much to get the same excellent results. The Occupational Outlook Handbook 2000-2001 (U.S. Department of Labor, 2000) reports that the median hourly wage for landscaping and groundskeeping laborers was $8.24. Another fairly good rule of thumb would be to offer at least $2 above minimum wage since it's hard to find unskilled jobs that pay that well.

However, according to industry experts and other business owners Entrepreneur spoke to, $10 an hour is about the going hourly rate for employees, which, compared to the current minimum wage looks pretty darned good. Some owners, like Steve M., a lawn care business owner in Minnesota who also does chemical applications, have a sliding wage scale. Steve's base wage is $10, but he pays more—around $12 an hour—to workers with certain qualifications, such as those with a spotless driving record or a pesticide certification.

> **Bright Idea**
>
> Schools and universities that have agriculture, landscape, or horticulture departments can be great sources of prospective employees. Not only are these students more likely to be interested in working in the field, but they'll also come to you with more knowledge about horticulture than the average person.

When you establish your base wage, keep in mind that in service industries like lawn care, it's not unusual for workers to change jobs to nab as little as a 25 cent per hour pay increase. So it's a good idea to ask around to see what other service providers are paying in your area and set your base pay rate accordingly.

"The truth is, this industry is starved for employees," says Tom Delaney, executive vice president of the Professional Lawn Care Association of America. "But the good news is, a mowing business needs fewer employees than other green businesses like landscaping. So your chances of finding enough people are not that bad."

The Chase Begins

Unless you have a few unemployed family members or neighbors positively panting for the chance to unleash your powerful beast of a mower on an unsuspecting lawn, you're going to have to do a little work to find qualified help. The classified ads of your local paper are the logical starting place for launching an employee search. The cost to advertise is usually fairly low, and you often can get a break on the price of the ad by running it several times. And make no mistake about it—you will have to run your ad more than once to smoke out the best candidates. Luckily, you don't need highly trained workers, but you do need reliable people who are willing to work hard. Having a bigger pool of candidates to draw from will allow you to choose more carefully. Take a look at a sample classified ad for a residential lawn care worker on page 74.

The people who are most likely to respond to your ad will be young, inexperienced, possibly uneducated, and possibly nonnative speaking. But that's not necessarily a bad

▲

Residential Lawn Care Worker

Part-time position for enthusiastic, reliable person who can handle large commercial lawn mower. No experience necessary—will train the right person. Competitive wages. Send letter of interest to:

Buzz Cuts

1142 Grandy Ave.

Munger, OR 97010

---

thing. Assuming your laborers are cooperative and eager to work (something you'll have to determine during an interview), you can teach them the right way (translation: your way) to do the job, and turn them into real pros.

Neither Nathan B., the owner who pays his workers so well, nor Albert T., the owner in Detroit, have had much luck finding hot prospects through the classifieds. Instead, they prefer to mine their employees, family, and friends for qualified candidates. Albert, for one, has found this approach to be very successful.

"I've been very lucky to find people through word-of-mouth who treat the job very professionally," he says. "That's important to me because my workers are a reflection on me."

Other areas where you may be able to unearth qualified help include any place you go where you personally get exceptional service, like at the gas station, convenience store, or restaurant; the professional organizations you belong to (other members may have college-age kids with time on their hands who need extra money); the local landscape or horticulture school or organization; and the local unemployment office, which may operate a job bank at no charge to you and the applicants.

Smart Tip

Tip...

Community newspapers are an excellent tool for unearthing prospective employees. Not only are their classified rates quite reasonable, but they're also read by people who live in the area where you do business. Their familiarity with your market area is a plus, and their proximity to your work site increases the chances they'll always be on time.

Giving 'em the Third Degree

Once you've identified a few promising prospects, you'll have to sit down with each one and determine his or her suitability for the job. Before the interview, have the candidate fill out a job application form, then refer to it as you ask questions. But don't just

Smart Tip

Tip...

In certain parts of the county, nonnative speakers make up a big part of the minimum wage worker pool. If you need help communicating with your Hispanic laborers, log on to www.freetranslation.com, where you can type in an English phrase or sentence and have it translated for you. Keep sentences as simple as possible for the most accurate translation.

talk—listen carefully to the person in front of you. You'll want to hire people who are enthusiastic, friendly, and articulate, as well as those with a strong work ethic. Experience is great, too—but don't pass up a good candidate just because he or she doesn't have on-the-job experience. Neophytes who receive good training can turn into good, cooperative, loyal employees.

You should also ask each candidate for a list of references, preferably compiled before the interview. Check these references carefully, because employees have been known to exaggerate on employment applications. In some cases, this can lead to disastrous results. (Imagine blithely trusting someone who claims to have hands-on experience with herbicides to service your commercial accounts, then finding out he was prevaricating when he fries your best customer's award-winning rose bushes.)

It's Not My Problem

If you're reconsidering this hiring thing, don't despair. If you're so inclined, you can turn over all the administrative details to a professional employer organization (PEO), a type of company that handles all the paperwork and other administrative functions. PEOs form a legal partnership with the business owner to handle his or her company's nonproductive employee administration activities, including human resources, payroll, government regulation compliance, taxes, and record-keeping. In essence, the PEO becomes the employer of record and "leases" the employee back to the business. The tradeoff is that the lawn service owner can then turn his or her attention solely to running and marketing the business.

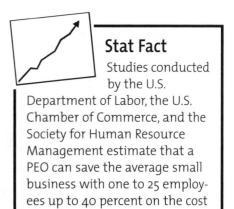

Stat Fact

Studies conducted by the U.S. Department of Labor, the U.S. Chamber of Commerce, and the Society for Human Resource Management estimate that a PEO can save the average small business with one to 25 employees up to 40 percent on the cost of workers' compensation and unemployment.

For tax reporting purposes, the business's employees fall under the PEO's federal tax ID and are recognized as its employees. PEOs often offer Fortune 500 benefits like

401(k) plans and cafeteria-style health insurance, thanks to the economies of scale a pool of hundreds or even thousands of workers can bring. Many PEOs will handle companies with as few as two or three employees at a cost that typically runs between 1.5 and 9 percent of the company's gross payroll. While that may sound steep, it can be a good bargain for owners who would rather have a root canal than deal with paperwork and government regulations.

The Employee Litmus Test

In many service industries, it's common to use independent contractors. You pay a flat fee for a person's services, and you don't withhold taxes, offer benefits or pay workers' compensation. While you might earn more profits this way, you could run afoul of the IRS, which has a 20-factor test to determine whether a person is an employee or a contractor. The penalties are steep if the IRS finds you're not in compliance. Here are the 20 factors:

Factor	Employee	Independent Contractor
Instructions	Complies with instructions regarding when, where, and how they work	Sets own rules
Training	Receives from employer	Obtains independently
Integration	Services are important to daily operations	Business can operate without services
Services	Completes work personally	Can hire others to do the work
Assistants	Doesn't hire, supervise, or pay assistants	Can hire own assistants
Relationship	Works on regular or recurring basis	Doesn't have continuing relationship
Schedule	Works hours set by employer	Works own hours
Hours worked	Works full time for one employer	Works for many employers
Location	Works on company premises	Doesn't have to work on premises

The Employee Litmus Test, continued

Factor	Employee	Independent Contractor
Work sequence	Follows instructions, routines	Doesn't follow set sequence
Reports	Accountable to employer for daily activities	Not accountable for daily tasks
Payment	Paid by hour, week, or month	Paid by the job
Expenses	Paid for by employer	Pays own overhead expenses
Tools and materials	Furnished by employer	Furnishes own
Investment	Has no investment in tools, facility used	Has significant investment in tools, facility used
Profit or loss	Not subject to losses	Makes profit or suffers loss
Number of employers	Works for one at a time	May work for many at a time
Service availability	Not available to others for work	Can work for multiple companies
Right to fire	Can be fired at any time of contract	Must be paid under terms
Right to quit	Can quit at any time	Must meet contract terms

8

Planting the
Seeds of Success

Just when you thought it was safe to water, BAM! The jaws of uncertainty open wide the moment you're faced with a unique situation or a problem you aren't sure how to handle. Maybe you're called on to repair the unsightly damage caused by overfertilization (caused by the homeowner's ex-lawn service provider, of course). Or you're unable to get a crucial part for your favorite mower (or edger or other power tool) in time to service your elaborate (and lucrative) country club account. Or maybe you've just run into a rough patch when it comes to collections and aren't comfortable strong-arming your clients.

This is where the professional development opportunities and information available through professional associations, industry publications, and university courses can be very helpful. These valuable resources can help you expand your general knowledge, spark new thinking and ideas, and keep you informed about industry developments. They're also valuable as a way to introduce you to "real world" situations and challenges. Finally, associations have an added benefit: They often permit you to use their official logo and name on your business cards, which is a signal to potential customers that you're a professional who takes your business seriously.

Here's a look at some of these professional resources.

Industry Associations

Lawn care industry associations can be some of your best resources in this business. It's up to you to investigate them all and decide which ones you need to belong to.

Associated Landscape Contractors of America

Founded in 1961, Virginia-based Associated Landscape Contractors of America (ALCA) offers technical and business management assistance, industry publicity, insurance, and networking opportunities to its members, most of whom are professional landscape contractors. Its quarterly publications are called *ALCA Advantage* and *ALCA In Depth*.

One of ALCA's most important benefits is its certification programs. The Certified Landscape Professional (Exterior and Interior) designation (CLP) is earned by passing a six-hour written test that covers business management topics. Certificate holders must recertify every three years by accumulating continuing education units of industry-related coursework or service. Those interested in the Exterior Certified Landscape Technician (CLT-E) certification must pass a hands-on field test with a choice of specialty area (maintenance, installation, or irrigation). Candidates must prove their competency with equipment, materials, and methods with an emphasis on safety. Finally, the Interior Certified Landscape Technician (CLT-I) designation can be earned by passing a four-hour written exam covering topics related to an interior technician's job duties.

The cost of the CLP certification is $150; the CLT certifications cost $75 each. A CLP study guide is available at $25 for ALCA members and $50 for nonmembers. See the ALCA Web site (www. alca.org) for details, including test dates and locations.

Membership dues in ALCA are $375 annually for companies with landscaping contracting business revenues of less than $250,000 per year (which would certainly include most start-ups—unless, of course, you have a really big first year!). The dues increase as revenues increase, topping out at $2,000 per year.

Beware!
Every state requires companies that offer lawn application services to be licensed. In addition, the person who actually applies the chemicals (including pesticides) must be certified. Contact your state department of agriculture for licensing requirements and certification testing.

Association of Professional Landscape Designers

The Association of Professional Landscape Designers (APLD) offers a national certification program that measures knowledge of design elements. You must be an APLD associate member in good standing and have a minimum of two years of landscape design experience to become certified. Other requirements include a minimum of 12 credit hours in landscape design courses and successful completion of the certification examination. Members are then permitted to use the APLD designation after their name. It should be mentioned that APLD does not offer an educational curriculum and instead recommends that courses be taken at accredited educational institutions such as universities, or at botanical gardens.

Recertification is required every three years and requires 30 continuing education unit contact hours, which can be earned though participation in any green industry event (including industry conferences, seminars, and classes).

Membership benefits include educational seminars, networking opportunities, publications (including the Designer and several other industry publications), and a speaker's bureau. Members also may purchase marketing brochures in bulk, such as "Guide to Hiring a Professional Designer," which is written for the consumer market.

Smart Tip
Tip...
Earning a certification through an industry association demonstrates to your customers that you take your business seriously and are up-to-date on the latest techniques and technologies the industry has to offer.

The dues for certified, associate, and allied members are $150 per year. Certified members also must pay a one-time $75 filing fee.

Landscape Maintenance Association Inc.

Based in Florida, the Landscape Maintenance Association Inc. (LMA) has a certification program for lawn maintenance technicians and managers that covers issues from horticulture management practices to tips for running a successful business. It also offers perks like insurance, workers' comp discounts, a Web site (www.floridayards.com), resource information, legislative action updates, and a newsletter. The membership cost for an individual with no employees is $125; the cost for businesses with one to five employees (including the owner) is $175; for six to 10 employees, it's $225.

Professional Lawn Care Association of America

Although primarily an association for the chemical lawn care industry, the Professional Lawn Care Association of America (PLCAA) also welcomes members in the lawn maintenance field. The association was organized in 1979 and offers a wide variety of educational opportunities, public outreach programs, and management development tools. Its annual conference, held in conjunction with the annual Green Industry Expo, takes place in November and features a full slate of educational courses and networking opportunities.

Important benefits this Georgia-based organization offers include insurance and retirement planning, legislative representation at the state and national levels, public awareness campaigns, and consumer brochures. It also provides industry certifications in Turfgrass Management (a home-study course offered in partnership with the University of Georgia) for $225 for members and $295 for nonmembers; and Landscape Tree and Shrub Maintenance, a PLCAA home-study course that's $195 for members and $225 for nonmembers.

PLCAA's publications include Pro Source, a quarterly newsletter, and a membership directory. It offers a wide range of marketing, management, and customer awareness tools, including books, videos, and CD-ROMs, many of which are available to nonmembers at a slightly higher cost. The cost to join the organization itself is $285 for companies with annual gross lawn care sales under $200,000; $500 for companies with sales of $200,000 to $599,999; and up. A company must be in business at least six months to be eligible to join.

Industry Publications

A good way to stay current on news, information, events, and trends in the lawn care service industry is by subscribing to publications that serve both the owner and the consumer. Here's a brief rundown of some of the best-known publications that can keep you plugged into this industry.

Trade Publications

Grounds Maintenance

Available free to landscape contractors, golf course, and recreational superintendents, and other landscape construction professionals, *Grounds Maintenance* is a monthly magazine that provides in-depth technical information and how-to insight. The easiest way to sign up is by accessing the subscription qualification form online at http://208.242.199.214/forms/subforms/gm.htm. Published by Intertec Publishing.

Landscape Management

This free monthly magazine provides a wealth of information to people in the green industry, including those involved in landscape management, athletic turf, "golfdom," and turfgrass in general. It also publishes a quarterly called *Athletic Turf* for sports turf managers and a newsletter called *Turfgrass Trends*. In addition, the magazine's Web site (www.landscapemanagement.net) provides extensive links to information on industry associations, disease management, turfgrass management, university programs, and current weather. The subscription qualification form can be found at www.advanstar.com/subscribe/lm/. Published by Advanstar Communications Inc.

Dollar Stretcher

Many lawn and landscape associations offer a wide range of membership benefits, including the use of the organization's logo in literature and advertising, merchant credit card acceptance programs, group rates on insurance, and even discounts on rental cars.

Lawn & Landscape

This monthly publication is the premier source for timely turfgrass news and information. Each issue tackles topics like residential mowing prices, proper pesticide application, add-on services that increase profits, and tips for sports field maintenance. A one-year subscription is $30 in the United States and $35 in Canada. Published by G.I.E. media.

PRO Magazine

This national trade magazine provides landscape professionals with timely business information. Its focus is on productivity, trends, and innovative techniques. It also has an e-mail forum at its Web site (www. promagazine.com). The subscription price is $48. Published eight times a year by Cygnus Business Media.

Turf Magazine

This magazine is written for professional landscape and mowing contractors, lawn care companies, chemical applicators, irrigation contractors, and landscape architects. Qualified business owners can receive the monthly publication free of charge. The online subscription form can be found at www.turfmagazine.com/sub scription.html. Published by Moose River Publishing LLC.

Consumer Publications

Better Homes and Gardens

Possibly the best known of the home and garden publications, this monthly magazine was founded in 1922 and boasts a circulation of 7.6 million. It has several major garden features in every issue. Published by Meredith Corp. Subscription price is $19 per year.

Flower & Garden Magazine

This magazine was established in 1956 and covers a wide range of gardening topics, from flower gardening to landscape design and lawn and landscape maintenance. A one-year subscription (six issues) is $19.95. Published by KC Publishing.

House & Garden

House & Garden is a high-style mix of objets d'art, eclectic furnishings, and tranquil, inspirational gardens. A subscription costs $15 per year. Published by Condé Nast Publications Inc.

Southern Living Garden Guide

Loaded with gardening tips and gorgeous photography, this annual magazine is a special publication of *Southern Living*, the venerable lifestyle publication that itself contains a wealth of home and garden tips. The 2001 garden edition had four articles about lawn care and a detailed U.S. growing guide. The magazine costs $4.99 on the newsstand. Its parent publication costs $19.97 for a one-year subscription. Published by Southern Living Inc.

University Courses

Quite a few universities across the United States have full-fledged turfgrass science programs that culminate in a bachelor of science degree. They're almost

> **Bright Idea**
> Annual trade shows and conventions are great places to network and gain knowledge. Besides workshops and seminars, they often have a trade show area where vendors and suppliers to the green industry ply their wares and services, allowing you to get up close and personal with the best and brightest in the business.

always offered through the schools' college of agriculture, so you're not likely to find such programs in urban schools. Some of these universities, like Ohio State and Penn State, also offer continuing education and "short courses" for lawn care professionals who wish to augment their knowledge of agriculture in general and turfgrass in particular without entering a formal degree program. Check with the school's agriculture department for information on these courses.

Albert T. in Detroit is one owner who appreciates the value of continuing education. In addition to earning a pesticide commercial license through the U.S. Department of Agriculture, he has taken classes and seminars in subjects like landscaping, irrigation, and outdoor lighting. He also is pursuing a bachelor of science degree in turfgrass management at Michigan State University.

Some of the universities in the United States that offer programs in turfgrass management and other related degrees include:

○ *Auburn University:* Turfgrass Management (College of Agriculture)

○ *Clemson University:* Turfgrass Management (College of Agriculture, Forestry, and Life Sciences)

○ *Cornell University:* Crop and Soil Sciences (New York State College of Agriculture & Life Sciences)

○ *Michigan State University:* Crop and Soil Sciences (College of Agriculture and Natural Resources)

○ *Ohio State University:* Turfgrass Science (College of Food, Agricultural, and Environmental Sciences)

○ *Pennsylvania State University:* Turfgrass Science (College of Agricultural Science)

○ *University of Florida:* Turfgrass Science (College of Agricultural and Life Sciences)

○ *University of Georgia:* Turfgrass Management (College of Agricultural and Environmental Sciences)

○ *University of Illinois:* Turfgrass Science and Management (College of Agricultural, Consumer, and Environmental Sciences)

○ *University of Kentucky:* Plant and Soil Science, Landscape Architecture (College of Agriculture)

You can find an extensive listing with additional turfgrass management degree programs on the Landscape Management Web site at www.landscape management.net.

▲

"A lot of clients are just as knowledgeable or even more knowledgeable about lawn care as the lawn guy is," Albert says. "Personally, I think that knowing about soil and grass makes me better at what I do."

Online Resources

Got a problem that has you stumped? If you have access to the Internet, you'll find a plethora of green industry online resources that can help. In addition to the wealth of knowledge available from associations and universities like the ones listed in this chapter, there are many Web sites, bulletin boards, and chat rooms you can log onto to get answers to your thorniest questions. Here are just a few of sites:

- *ALCA:* www.alca.org (with a members-only bulletin board, professional development links, referrals, classified marketplace)
- *APLD:* www.apld.org/educational.html (extensive green industry education database)
- *Cyberlawn:* www.opei.org (offers a guide to power equipment, mower maintenance info, and links to other lawn and garden information; sponsored by the Outdoor Power Equipment Institute)
- *GrassMasters Lawn Service Forum:* www.ezboard.com (lawn service information resources and bulletin board)
- *Grounds Maintenance:* http://industry click.com ("textbook" information on turf-grass and propagation, with links to the periodical's articles)
- *Landscape Management*: www.landscape management.net (links to national and international associations, and information on diseases, environmental issues, general turfgrass issues, and more. It also has a listing of university programs in turfgrass management.)
- *Lawn & Landscape Magazine:* www.lawnandlandscape.com (message board)
- *Lawnservicing.com:* www.lawnservicing.com (another GrassMasters site with extensive links to industry publications, equipment resources, tutorials, government sites, and business strategies)
- *Lawnsite.com:* www.lawnsite.com (message board for commercial lawn and snow plowing discussions)

9

Spreading
the Word

In the musical "Hello Dolly!" Dolly Levi exclaims:
"Money—pardon my expression—is like manure; it's not worth a
thing unless it's spread about encouraging young things to grow."
That also essentially sums up the theory behind advertising.

Basically, you have to spend money to make money. Businesses advertise regularly because they want to reach their audience as quickly and expediently as possible to showcase new products, tout innovative services, and establish a corporate image. Small businesses advertise because their livelihood and longevity depend on it.

This chapter examines a number of advertising techniques that can be used to make your business the top-of-mind choice for customers who are seeking a quality lawn care company.

Timing Is Everything

Your main advertising campaign should be launched right before the last frost or heavy winter rains, which usually occur in late February or March. (Since meteorology isn't an exact science, try looking at seasonal weather data for the past 20 years or so to get an idea of when you can expect winter's last gasp in your region.) This is when homeowners start longing for spring and begin to make decisions about spring landscaping and mowing services. The trick is to advertise aggressively at that point and pick up enough business to carry you through the busy summer months.

Your Plan of Attack

Before you start dropping dollars on advertising of any kind, it's wise to create a basic marketing plan. This plan doesn't have to be complicated, but it should be detailed enough to serve as a road map that keeps your business on track and your marketing efforts on target. In addition, it should be updated periodically as market conditions change so you're always in touch with the needs of your customers.

Your marketing plan can be a part of the business plan you've already written. (Refer back to Chapter 4 for information about business plans.) It should describe your target market and the competitive environment you're operating in, as well as discuss how you're going to make your customers aware of your business. Information related to pricing, industry trends, and advertising also have a place in your marketing plan.

SWOT Analysis

An integral part of the marketing plan is your SWOT analysis. SWOT stands for Strengths (characteristics that make you special and set you apart from the competition), Weaknesses (things you need to overcome that your competitors could take advantage of), Opportunities (anything you can do that might benefit your business either now or in the future), and Threats (anything that can harm your business).

Bigger Fish to Fry

Once you've been in business for a while and feel you can easily handle the rigors of running the show on all fronts, it might be time to expand—either by taking on more residential customers or by dipping your toe into the waters of commercial business. If you opt for the latter, you'll need to refine your marketing efforts somewhat since marketing to businesses requires a more sophisticated approach.

Kick off your sales efforts to office complexes, churches, municipal parks, and other public areas by sending a brief business letter to your prospects (each one personalized using a word processing mail merge program). Remind them of the value of well-kept grounds in terms of corporate image and property value, then point out how an outside lawn service is much more cost-effective than having a person on staff. Also emphasize the things that make your service unique (and better than the competition) in case they use an outside service but are considering switching. Then after a week or so, make a follow-up call to request an appointment with the business owner or facilities manager.

At the appointment, give an informal presentation on your services. Include information like the labor cost savings a lawn care business can bring, the advantages of a well-kept lawn, and so on. Also, show pictures of some of the lawns you're currently servicing (but be sure to ask the homeowners' permission before photographing their properties). Mount your presentation in a sales presentation case (available at office supply stores), which has pages inside for your pictures and documents and stands up like an easel. Stress your reliability and professionalism, then offer a list of references, certifications (if any), and a business card and/or brochure.

After a few days, follow up with a phone call, politely reiterating your request to serve the client. The answer won't always be "yes," but don't get discouraged. Rejection is part of selling, and with persistence and continued professionalism, the response may one day be affirmative.

Putting these characteristics on paper will give you a snapshot of your business's prospects.

On page 90, we've included a sample SWOT analysis for a new lawn care business in a medium-sized urban area of about 30,000 people. Try creating your own SWOT analysis by using the blank form on page 91. You also can use the SWOT approach to analyze the strengths and weaknesses of your competition to see how you stack up

▲

SWOT Analysis	
Strengths Two summers working for a landscape contractor My strong business background (B.A. in business administration) My strong communication skills—I can schmooze with anyone	**Weaknesses** No experience with advertising or marketing Computer-illiterate (Must learn accounting software!) Allergic to pollen (Note to myself: See doc for allergy prescription)
Opportunities No other lawn services located within five-mile radius New condos under construction on Ferris that might be source of future income	**Threats** Commercial landscaper on Park St. is now accepting residential mowing customers Rumors that city is considering prohibiting homebased businesses because of past abuses

against them. Once you've created your SWOT analysis, refer to it often as a guide for addressing the weaknesses you've identified and as a benchmark against which you can judge your successes.

Read All About It

Another important part of your marketing plan is your promotion strategy. Every lawn care professional, from the one-man band who juggles a dozen or so jobs a week to the person who needs a staff to help handle the workload, must advertise to get new business.

The types of advertising that are most effective for lawn service companies include Yellow Pages ads, business cards, fliers, direct mail, word-of-mouth, and newspaper ads. You'll find each of these discussed below.

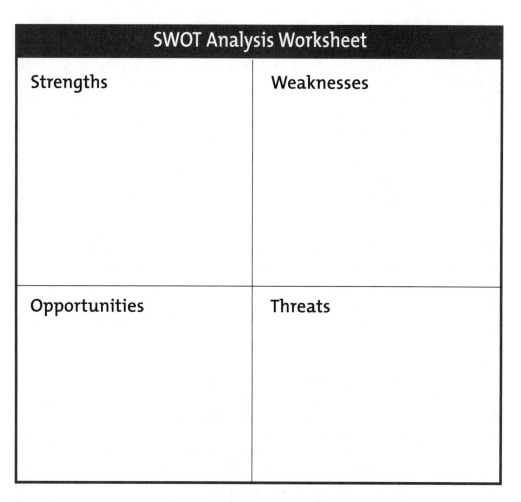

SWOT Analysis Worksheet	
Strengths	**Weaknesses**
Opportunities	**Threats**

Yellow Page Ads

Looking for a maintenance-free advertising vehicle that never closes, gets lost, or breaks down? Then you've come to the right place with a listing in the Yellow Pages. There's no monthly charge to list your business in this reliable old workhorse because you automatically receive a simple line ad when your business telephone service is activated.

Your basic listing will be published under a heading like "Lawn Maintenance" and normally will contain only your company name, address, and telephone number. These days, some directories will also list your Web or e-mail address for an additional fee, which is usually worth the extra cost.

If you prefer, you can place a display ad. This type of ad is usually boxed and is much larger than a line ad. But as impressive as it might look when you open the directory, a display ad isn't really particularly useful for a lawn care business, according to the owners Entrepreneur spoke to. After all, your business is seasonal, but you'll be contracted to pay for the ad for the whole year. But if you decide to buy a display ad, examine the directory listings carefully to make sure there's a clear category heading your customers can find easily. Also, check to see if your competition places display ads. If not, that's a pretty strong indication that it's not necessary to spend the money to attract customers.

Display ads can be very pricey—often hundreds of dollars per month based on a 12-month contract with no escape clause. You sign up, you're committed.

Lowell P. in Stanwood, Washington, pays $175 a year for a display ad in his local phone directory. It includes clip art of a shovel and rake, which he feels makes the ad stand out among the others on the page. "An ad is important for me because 80 percent of the people who have homes [in my community] don't live here full time," says Lowell, who lives on an island known for its beauty and remote location.

You might think that placing a display ad when everyone else has a line ad would be a great way to grab attention. But that's not necessarily so, according to Barbara Koch, author of Profitable Yellow Pages (FTD Association). "Many small-business owners buy more ad space than they need," Koch says. "Yellow Page ads are effective because advertisers have a captive audience who have already made a decision to buy. But that's also what makes it unnecessary to buy a display ad in most cases. The real role of your ad is to get the customer to choose you over someone else, and factors like your location may be what actually causes them to call you."

To place a Yellow Pages ad or for more information, call the publisher of the directory you wish to advertise in.

Smart Tip
When writing your marketing plan, think about every time you'll interact with your customers. This includes personal contact, e-mail, and even the invoices you'll send. Each contact should be considered a potential marketing opportunity.

Business Cards

Business cards are a great way to advertise at a very low cost. Those little rectangles of paper are not only your calling card, but they also remind a prospective customer that you're only a phone call away when he or she is ready to commit to hiring you. As a result, you should distribute your card freely wherever you go, including to anyone who should happen to walk up to you while you're on a job site with your mower in full throttle. (Keep a supply in your truck rather than on you, since they can get bent or soiled.)

As we mentioned in Chapter 6, these little workhorses are really quite inexpensive—only about $35 for 1,000 cards. Although you can make up your own by buying a pack of computer-printable business cards, it's

Beware!

You may need a permit to go door-to-door legally in your community. Check with the city or township clerk's office, then be sure to carry the permit in your pocket while you're pounding the pavement. You may have to pay a small fee for the permit.

really more cost-effective (not to mention less labor-intensive) to pony up the dough for professionally printed cards. In a pinch, though (like if your regular supply runs out), the printable ones are fine.

In addition to giving your company name and contact information on your card, it's helpful to include descriptive words like "reliable" and credentials like "certified." And while people usually expect you to give them an estimate without charge, printing "Free Estimates" on your cards is still a good idea because the word "free" is such a powerful motivator.

Once you have your newly printed cards in hand, it's time to hit the bricks and get them out to the masses. Set aside several hours at a time for the distribution effort, and be sure to wear your company shirt or other clean, presentable attire when you canvass the neighborhoods so you look professional and competent. Never place anything in a homeowner's or business's mailbox. That is an invasion of the person's privacy and is a punishable federal offense. No kidding.

Some of the market segments that might be ripe prospects for your services include homeowners, businesses, real estate brokers, home and garden stores, and lawn mower repairpersons.

Obviously, homeowners are your biggest target market and the place where you should distribute the most cards. The most direct approach for reaching homeowners is by going door to door. You don't have to knock on the door or speak to each homeowner. Just tape your card to the door or screen handle where it can't be missed.

If the resident comes to the door while you're doing the deed, hand the card to him or her instead and make a brief, courteous pitch about your skills and reliability. While you're at it, ask if the person knows anyone who's looking for a lawn service. That could result in an immediate job.

Any time you go door-to-door, be sure to have estimate forms and a measuring wheel stashed in your truck just in case the homeowner asks for an on-the-spot

Bright Idea

Cable TV is another place where your marketing dollars will go far. Since cable systems serve relatively small, local markets, placing an ad on the local cable station's "bulletin board" practically guarantees it will be seen by precisely the people you're trying to reach. Call the system's sales department for advertising rates before you pay to produce an ad.

estimate. Never let a live one get away by making him or her wait until you can return with the appropriate tools.

Another fairly easy way to distribute your card is to enlist the help of the newspaper in your community who, for a fee, will tuck your card into the paper. Alternately, you could ride along with a newspaper carrier and insert the cards yourself at each stop. In any event, put the card deeply between pages two and three of the front section so it can't fall out and won't be overlooked by the reader. If the paper has been inserted into a poly bag before delivery, you can slip the card inside the bag. But since the card can be lost when the paper is pulled from the bag, it's always better to place it between the pages of the paper.

While you're out canvassing the neighborhood, be sure to stop by buildings occupied by professional people like doctors, dentists, attorneys, and insurance agents, and leave your card with the receptionist. Although these professionals may already have a service handling the lawn work, they may be in the market for someone new in the future. Ask the receptionist to keep your card on file just in case.

Real estate brokers could be a mother lode of new, though fluctuating, business. Real estate brokers often sell homes for owners who have relocated to other cities or states and need a reliable mowing service—if not now, then in the future. By the same token, some real estate brokers offer relocation services and look after the homes of absentee owners. Get your card into the hands of these brokers either by stopping by in person or by mailing it along with a carefully worded sales letter. You'll find a sample letter on page 99.

They may carry a dizzying array of home and garden tools for do-it-yourselfers (including—oh, no!—lawn care equipment), but home and garden stores are still potential distribution points for your business card. Make arrangements with the store owner or manager to leave a supply of your cards on the counter near the cash register for any lawn-impaired customer who might prefer to hire a professional like you. Better still, provide a business card holder with the cards to keep them neat and tidy on the counter.

Here's another one of those transient sources of work that really can add up to big bucks: People who take their mowers to a lawn mower repair service will be unable to tend their own lawns while the beast is out of commission—and that can be for weeks at a time during the busy season. The result? You can easily step in and cash in on an interim basis. Best of all, some of these temporary customers can turn into regulars. So stop by to introduce yourself to the lawn mower repairperson in your community and leave a supply of cards that can be distributed to mowerless customers. Check the Yellow Pages under categories like "Lawn Mowers," "Lawn Mowers—Sharpening and Repairing," "Lawn Mower Engines," and "Engines—Gasoline" to find the names of all the repair shops in your community.

Fliers

Simple to create and inexpensive to produce, fliers are probably the second hardest-working weapon in your advertising arsenal. Like business cards, fliers can be distributed widely at a fairly low cost—as little as eight cents each when reproduced by a quickie print shop like American Speedy Printing. Fliers are generally one-sided on letter-sized paper, and can be folded and placed under windshield wipers in parking lots, posted on bulletin boards at the mall or supermarket, or distributed door-to-door. To increase the effectiveness of your flier, staple a business card to each one, since people are more apt to file away a business card for future reference than a piece of paper.

You can save money by using a word processing program like Microsoft Word to design the flier. (Try using Word's "Flier Wizard" to make the job easier.) Make it as appealing and easy-to-read as possible by using white space, call-outs like bullets or lists, and no more than one or two typefaces (any more than that and your flier will look like a ransom note). Among the things to stress in your flier are your reliability (a BIG one), your professionalism, the conveniences you offer, and the pride customers will have when they see their beautiful lawn.

It's not necessary, however, to give prices in your flier. Generate interest by using terms like "reasonable rates," then give a phone number where you can be reached.

Lowell P. uses a variation on the flier idea to informally advertise his business. He creates a "Lowell Says" flier on his home computer that that gives tips on growing flowers or preventing pests, then posts them on all the free bulletin boards available in the small rural communities around his home. He says the fliers have really helped to make his name known in the community.

You'll find a sample flier on page 100.

Closely related to fliers are postcards, which, like business cards, are sometimes more likely to find their way into an address book or a planner than a flier. Chris B. in Tyler, Texas, has been very successful advertising his chemical lawn service using postcards. His postcard features pictures of a beautifully tended lawn and a weedy lawn on one side, and a list of his services on the other. "We've worn out the shoe leather putting our postcards on doors," he says. "We also just mailed 1,700 of them at a cost of $480 to one of the gated communities in the area, and the responses are already starting to come in."

▲

Bright Idea

Sending a sales letter to your local board of realtors or chamber of commerce can be an easy way to drum up new business. Be sure to use postage on the envelopes (so they don't look like junk mail), and mail them just before the start of the mowing season since this is when people will be most receptive to trying a new service.

Direct Mail

Another way to reach potential customers right where they live is with direct mail, which is any promotional piece you send through the mail. This can include everything from brochures to newsletters and coupon books. (We'll discuss brochures and other marketing tools in Chapter 11.) Your direct mail piece doesn't have to be elaborate; a simple letter or flier with the appropriate hard-hitting sales copy will do. You'll also want to include a mail-back card (prepaid only—otherwise the chances of it being returned are very slim) or a business card to make it easy for your reader to contact you.

The biggest challenge with direct mail is getting the customer to actually open the envelope it comes in. So there are a few tricks you can use to incite their curiosity about the contents. One is to put the mailer in a plain No. 10 envelope that has only a return address (but no company name). This gives the envelope the appearance of personal correspondence. But be sure to affix first-class postage to the envelope—bulk postage is a dead giveaway that the missive inside is advertising.

Another trick that works well is using a teaser line on the envelope that piques the reader's interest. "Free" and "Increase your property value now!" are the type of teasers that would work well for a lawn care business. As mentioned earlier, the word "free" is a powerful motivator, so offer a deal like one or two free mowings with a prepaid payment for three months of service to encourage more people to respond.

There's one more type of direct mail piece that bears mentioning here. That's marriage mail, which is a package that contains advertising fliers or coupons from a number of different advertisers. They're usually sized to fit a No. 10 or a business-sized envelope and are often printed in full color on glossy paper. The advantage is that this type of package is usually quite cost-effective, since you're only paying for a percentage of the "ride." The disadvantage is that your flier will be accompanied by other fliers from nail technicians, chiropractors, dry cleaners, and possibly other lawn services. But the low cost usually outweighs the disadvantages. To find a company that specializes in marriage mail in your target market, look in the Yellow Pages under headers like "Advertising—Coupons," "Advertising—Direct Mail," and "Sales Promotion Service."

Word-of-Mouth

Whoever said there's no such thing as a free lunch must have overlooked word-of-mouth (WOM) advertising. Not only is the price right, but WOM praise is one of the most powerful advertising vehicles you have at your disposal. One of its major advantages is that you often don't have to do anything special to garner this kind of freebie publicity. All you do is perform your job to the best of your ability, and people will talk favorably about you and your willingness to do whatever it takes to satisfy the customer.

The key to getting good WOM is influencing what your customers say about you. You can do this in a number of ways. Some lawn service owners call their clients a few weeks into the mowing season to get feedback and verify their satisfaction. Doing this projects a positive image of you and your company because it's so rare for business-people in service industries to follow up after the sale. You might also get a referral or two from the satisfied homeowner during the conversation, which you can turn into a WOM opportunity by using his or her name when you call the person to whom you were referred.

Another way to influence WOM is by doing something positive and visible in your community or on the home and garden circuit. For example, you could present a complimentary instructional seminar on lawn care techniques for kids at the local youth center who are interested in making a few bucks mowing lawns (and who are definitely not much competition for you), and invite the local media to attend. Any coverage you get is bound to focus not only on your benevolence, but also on the services you offer. That can lead to new business.

A third way to use WOM to your advantage is to offer a referral reward program to existing customers. Mike A. in South Dakota has acquired plenty of new business by giving a 10 percent discount off a month's worth of mowing for referrals made in his service area.

 Beware!
Bad word-of-mouth can be devastating for a start-up business. Experts say that a dissatisfied customer might not complain to you but will tell six to seven people about the bad experience. So if you suspect that a client isn't happy with you, do whatever you can to find out why and fix the problem. The future of your business could depend on it.

Newspaper Ads

You'll notice we haven't said much about newspaper advertising. Some entrepreneurs, like Bill V. in Urbana, Illinois, who advertise for a few weeks in the daily newspaper at the start of the mowing season, feel the ads unearth some new business. Lowell P. in

Washington says he pretty much launched his business with four $8 ads in the local newspaper. But most of the other owners we spoke to didn't think paid advertising—including classifieds—in daily newspapers was worth the cost. But if your community has a free weekly shopper, you might have a go at it. The advertising in these papers tends to be quite inexpensive, and the biggest payoff seems to come from the local business and professional service section. People like to frequent the businesses in their own community and might look favorably on engaging your services.

Sales Letter

MOWING MASTERS

25771 Regal Drive
Kissimmee, Florida 34741
(555) 555-5555

Dear Homeowner:

It's almost spring—time to spruce up your home to make it look as fresh and beautiful as the new season. But if you're like most people, you're constantly on the go, rushing to business meetings, taking the kids to soccer and baseball practice, running errands, and doing all the other things it takes to run a career and a home. So you probably don't have as much time as you'd like to devote to the upkeep of your lawn and shrubs.

That's where Mowing Masters can help. We're a full-service lawn maintenance company located right here in your neighborhood. In addition to basic lawn mowing, we provide other quality services like hedge and bush trimming, fertilizing, thatching, and aerating—everything you need to make your home the showplace of your block.

We're experienced, reliable, and reasonably priced. You don't even have to sign a seasonal contract with Mowing Masters to get our best rates. We'll be happy to bill you monthly. And of course, your satisfaction is 100 percent guaranteed.

Please call (555) 555-5555 today for a free estimate. Call by March 15 and you'll receive a 10 percent discount on your first month of mowing as a token of our thanks.

Sincerely,

Dan Williams
Owner

MOWING MASTERS

25771 Regal Drive
Kissimmee, Florida 34741
(555) 555-5555

FULL-SERVICE LAWN MOWING

For the house you love to come home to!

Reliable, reasonably priced residential services include:

- ❏ Mowing and Edging
- ❏ Fertilizing
- ❏ Trimming
- ❏ Aerating
- ❏ Thatching

Call for a free on-site consultation and estimate.

(555) 555-5555

10

Increasing Power
with the Internet

If you were asked to name the one innovation that has impacted people around the world more than anything else in the last decade, chances are you'd say "the Internet" without hesitation.

Photo ©PhotoDisc Inc.

The Internet truly has revolutionized the way America and its global neighbors do business. As a result, being connected to the Internet through an ISP, or Internet service provider, has become as important for businesses as having electricity or a telephone.

In fact, being online is no longer an option—it's an economic necessity. The Internet gives us instant access to important information like NFL stats for the team that holds the record for the most consecutive games lost (as of this writing, Tampa Bay, 1976–77, 26 games) and shows us "live cam" shots of places like the summit of Alaska's Mt. McKinley during a snowstorm. But more important, the Internet has given us the world. Quite literally, in fact, since at the click of a mouse, we can now communicate 24/7 with people and businesses in the outer reaches of the planet.

According to the online statistical resource eMarketer, 81 million people age 35 to 54 (many of whom are homeowners) were surfing the Web in 1999. An additional 64 million people in the 18-to-34 age group were online that same year. Small wonder, then, that revenues garnered through online advertising increased from $900 million in 1997 to $1.9 billion in 1998, according to the Internet Advertising Bureau.

So what does all this mean to you, the owner of a start-up lawn care business? It means you can get a lot of visibility without a whole lot of effort. It also means that you cannot overlook the power of the Internet, both as a resource for your own business and as an electronic pathway for your customers. That bears repeating. You must

Fun Fact

The idea for the Internet was first conceived in the 1960s as a way to link the Department of Defense with other parts of the military. The Defense Advanced Research Projects Agency is credited with establishing the first rudimentary Web.

be online these days because consumers have become so accustomed to having information immediately and whenever they want it. Many of these consumers will surf the Net to find answers and leads to products and services like yours. And if you're not out there when they're looking, they'll definitely go somewhere else.

Although nearly all the business owners Entrepreneur spoke with did not yet have a Web site on the Internet, all recognized the value of this tool and expressed an interest in getting out into cyberspace eventually. So what's stopping them now? Lack of time, not lack of interest. Even though few of them would even consider creating their own sites, all were interested in providing substantial input into the Web site that will represent them in cyberspace. So you should give very serious thought to getting a Web site up and running as soon as you can.

This chapter will not teach you the basics of surfing the Web. We will assume that you know how to log onto an ISP, use a search engine, and send and retrieve e-mail. Instead, it will discuss how the Internet can help you run your company and capture new business at the same time. But if, by chance, you haven't explored the power of the Internet yet, you simply must become acquainted with this valuable resource right away. Community colleges and adult education programs are excellent places to learn about using the Web. There are also many books and software packages on the market that can walk you through the basics of e-mail, surfing, and Web site development.

A Phenomenal Resource

Before we delve into a discussion of using the Internet as an electronic business card, we'll first explore its value as a resource and problem-solver. This amazing tool can help you locate everything from advice on treating snow mold on northern lawns to the address of a repair shop across the country that carries a part you need right now. You can do market research, investigate local zoning ordinances, and get tax help. And you can accomplish all this any time of the day or night, all without leaving the comfort of your office.

Another advantage of the Internet is the small-business opportunities and advice that can be accessed. There are a number of chat rooms and bulletin boards specifically for lawn care business owners where you can share tips and trade information (we listed some of them in Chapter 8). There are also quite a few sites in cyberspace

Stat Fact
International Data Research predicts that the Internet economy will top $2.8 trillion by 2003.

where small-business owners can find ideas to help them do business better. One to check out is *Entrepreneur* magazine's site at www.entrepreneur.com.

There's no charge for most of the wisdom out there beyond the cost of server connection fees to access the Web. But remember: Sometimes you get exactly what you pay for. Just as you don't always believe everything you see in print or on the evening news, you shouldn't necessarily believe everything that's posted on the Internet. After all, anyone and everyone who has the bucks to build a Web site, from prison inmates to the president of the Smooth River Stone Association of America, can launch themselves into cyberspace and say whatever they want. So, as the saying goes, caveat emptor, or "Let the buyer beware."

To protect yourself, always consider the source when searching for information, and stick with the most reputable people or companies. Let's say, for instance, you're looking for tax planning advice. You know you can trust the information you find on *Entrepreneur* magazine's site rather than a Web site called "Manny's Guide to Beating the IRS."

As mentioned previously, the Internet is also an excellent place to start your search for lawn care and office supplies and equipment. Although not every company has its own Web site, there's been a huge proliferation of new Web sites in the past few years. As a result, it's likely you'll find the larger service companies, such as vehicle and equipment manufacturers, out in cyberspace and thus at your beck and call. (You'll find some of them listed in the Appendix and in "Straight to the Source" on pages 108 and 109.)

Work It

Here are a few other ways to use the Internet:
- Seek help with lawn maintenance problems
- Research new mower and other product purchases
- Locate professional development courses
- Keep tabs on the competition
- Check the weather forecast
- Research turf diseases and remedies
- Purchase books and other reference/educational materials
- Buy and sell used equipment

Being connected through the Internet also helps you communicate better (and often faster, since you don't waste time playing phone tag). You can place orders with suppliers, then check on their status whenever you like. You can also keep in closer touch with your customers, who may find it more convenient to e-mail you instead of picking up the phone to tell you they'd like an extra service like fertilizing or hedge trimming.

"I often work by e-mail with my clients," says one resourceful business owner in Ohio. "It's much easier to send off an e-mail than to write a letter, and it's cheaper than a phone call. I may also receive an answer back the same day. You cannot beat e-mail for efficiency."

Your Cyber Salesperson

Just as you can access other companies' Web sites for information about their products and services, you'll want prospective customers to find you in cyberspace, too. That means that establishing your Web site should be high on your list of priorities as you start your business. But you don't have to be an information technology whiz or a computer programmer to get the job done. There are many do-it-yourself Web page kits on the market that almost anyone can figure out. But before we start the exciting process of building your company Web site, let's take a look at the Web site development process.

Back to Basics

Because your Web site is virtual advertising that's available on demand 24 hours a day, it's important to spend a fair amount of time considering what it should say. You can do this by thinking like a customer and answering the questions you think he or she would have when searching for a lawn care service. Here are examples of the kinds of questions your customer might have:

- How long have you been in business?
- What do you charge?
- Are edging and trimming included in your base rate?
- When will you cut my lawn if it rains on my regularly scheduled day?
- What other types of services do you provide (e.g., fertilizing and chemical services)?
- Do you charge for estimates?
- How will I pay you?
- Do you have references?
- How can I reach you?
- How soon can you start?

Armed with answers to these questions, you should next consider how you want the site to look. It should be clean, uncluttered, and easy to use. You'll also want to keep the copy brief because many people find it annoying to have to keep scrolling down as they read. In addition, Web surfers tend to have short attention spans and won't hesitate to click off your site.

Building a Better Web Site

The next decision you must make relates to the type of Web site you want to build. A simple option is the online business card, which is no more than a single screen that gives your company name and contact information like your address, phone number, and fax number. This type of Web site is actually quite easy to build, even for those who don't know a byte from a baud. There are many how-to Internet books available in bookstores or from online retailers like Amazon.com that can guide you through the process of creating your own page. However, the disadvantage of this kind of Web page is there's not much room for information. If you want to make a sales pitch (and why else would you go to the trouble of creating a site?), you should consider creating an online "brochure" instead.

With an online brochure, you can answer questions like the ones listed earlier, and provide links to your e-mail inquiry form and other pertinent information. This is also a good way to discuss the various services you offer in detail rather than just listing them.

Romancing the Home(page)

By now you've probably realized that because your expertise lies in caring for the green, green grass of home, you'll want to hire a professional Web designer to create your Web page. As mentioned above, you can design it yourself using a how-to book. But unless you're well-versed in both HTML and graphic design, it's probably more trouble than it's worth, especially when there are experienced professionals out there who are awaiting your call.

Because Web designers quite often are also graphic designers, they'll want you to work with them to make decisions about content, copy placement, colors, typefaces, and so on. But you can feel confident relying on the designer's best judgment when it comes to level of interactivity, navigation tools, and artwork.

Designers charge $800 to $4,000 for Web site design. Part of this cost is based on the number of pages on the site. The more complex it is, the more it costs.

If you really think you can handle HTML and Web site development yourself, try using a Web page layout program like Dreamweaver by Macromedia (retails for $299, available from www.macromedia.com) or Microsoft FrontPage (retails for $149.99, available from www.compusa.com). Microsoft Word also has an HTML conversion feature that can translate your prose into computerese.

Selecting a Domain Name

Like your company, your Web site has to have a unique name that will be used on the server on which it resides. This is called the domain name, or URL. Examples of lawn-related domains include "gogreenlawns. com" and "yardking.com." Using your business name as your domain name is usually your best bet, but keep in mind that domain names must be unique, and someone else might already be using the name you've chosen.

You have to register your domain name to get exclusive use of it. Domain names are registered for a minimum of two years at a cost of approximately $70. They can be renewed by paying another registration fee when they expire. There are several companies that handle registration, but the best-known is domain.com, which also allows you to register your name for five- or 10-year periods. The cost for these longer registrations is $30 and $25 per year, respectively.

The Host with the Most

The last thing you have to do to go live on the Net is to select an Internet host site. This is where your site will "reside" so users can access it 24 hours a day. Examples of well-known Internet hosts include Microsoft Network and Prodigy, but there are many, many smaller hosts around the country. Before selecting a host, ask other businesspeople for recommendations. You'll want to know how often the host site goes down and how long it takes to fix it, whether it has reliable customer support, how many incoming lines the server has (so users don't get a lot of busy signals when they call), and how big it is.

A caveat is in order here. Remember those prison inmates we mentioned earlier? Even they can be Web hosts if they can somehow get the right computer equipment and telephone trunk lines installed in their cell block. Unfortunately, if you take a chance with a lesser-known host, you run the risk of having it go out of business or disappearing in the night, which will not inspire confidence in your customers.

Web hosting prices start as low as $14.95 per month for 100MB of disk space. Some hosts also will allow you to register your domain name. Web hosting is very competitive, so it pays to shop around. You'll find the names of a few companies you can investigate in the Appendix.

Straight to the Source

Here are some Web sites you can use to do business better and find useful (free) advice:

❑ Amazon.com: sells books, CDs, videos, and more (www.amazon.com)

❑ Business Planning Resource: tips for business start-ups, as well as sample business and marketing plans (www.plans.com)

❑ Business Resource Center: a site for financing, marketing, and management information (www.imswest.com)

❑ Census Bureau: the official government Web site for statistics and demographics (www.census.gov)

❑ Entrepreneur: the premier source for small-business advice (www.entrepreneur.com)

❑ FindLaw: a source for legal resources (www.findlaw.com)

❑ GardenNet: interesting information regarding plants and garden equipment, plus shopping resources (www.gardennet.com)

❑ Honda Power Equipment: mowers and other power equipment (www.hondapowerequipment.com)

❑ IRS: official source for tax tips and advice (www.irs.ustreas.gov)

❑ John Deere: information about the company's walk-behind and riding mowers (www.johndeere.com)

❑ Landscape Management: green industry publication for landscapers (www.landscapegroup.com)

❑ Lawn Institute: Turfgrass Producers' International member site (www.lawninstitute.com)

❑ Mapquest: online driving directions in the United States (www.mapquest.com)

❑ Marketing Resource Center: valuable tips for small-business owners (www.marketingsource.com)

❑ Marketing Tips: a source for Internet-based marketing information (www.marketingtips.com)

❑ National Association for the Self-Employed: offers advice, group insurance, and more (www.nase.org)

Straight to the Source, continued

❑ National Association of Enrolled Agents: a source for locating accountants (www.naea.org)

❑ National Association of Home Based Businesses: tips and information for homebased businesses (www.usahomebusiness.com)

❑ National Small Business Network: interactive resource for home office and small-business owners (www.businessknowhow.net)

❑ Outdoor Power Equipment Institute: earth-friendly lawn care tips, mower maintenance information, and links to other useful sites (www.opei.org)

❑ Professional Lawn Care Association of America: lawn care tips for members and the general public (www.plcaa.org)

❑ Scag Power Equipment: manufacturer of commercial lawn equipment (www.scag.com)

❑ Small Business Administration: the small-business owner's best friend with extensive FAQs and advice (www.sbaonline.sba.gov)

❑ Small Office: a site with articles and advice for small business (www.smalloffice.com)

❑ Snapper: products and lawn care tips (www.snapper.com)

❑ Toro Co.: mowers and outdoor maintenance products (www.toro.com)

11

Blowing
Your Own Horn

Between your paid advertising efforts and your Web site, you should be able to spread the word about your new business pretty efficiently and effectively. But as you know, advertising costs money—and that's something you may not have in overabundance in the early days of your new venture.

Fortunately, there are some marketing and public relations tools you can incorporate into your promotional mix at a relatively low cost. Among these tools are newsletters, feature articles, home and garden show promotions, and networking. Here's a rundown of how each one can generate positive publicity for your business.

Newsletters

Ever since the advent of desktop publishing in the 1990s, it seems like everyone—from state senators to local florists—is sending out a newsletter. And with good reason. Newsletters are easy to create, they're inexpensive to produce, and they're very effective for delivering a copious amount of targeted information to your best prospects.

Informational newsletters tend to work best for lawn care professionals. A typical newsletter might contain checklists ("Ways To Wake Up Your Lawn This Spring"), information about the optimal time for the first spring cutting, facts about the different types of fertilizer and the importance of a regular fertilization program, information about the best way to trim hedges and shrubs, and so on. Obviously, you'll want to tailor the content to reflect your business specialties, since the idea here is to subtly sell your services while providing useful tips to the prospect. You can do this by adding a tag line to the end of each story that touts your expertise. For example, on the fertilizing story, you could end with a line that says something like, "The Cutting Edge can start you on a fertilization schedule that will keep your lawn green and pristine all season long. Call (800) 555-5555 for a no-obligation quote."

Mailing a single newsletter just before the beginning of the growing season is sufficient for a business that focuses on mowing alone. If you also plan to do chemical applications, you might want to send another newsletter at the end of the season when people are starting to think about winterizing their lawns.

Writing and Producing a Newsletter

Your newsletter should be written in a concise, journalistic style, which means each story should answer the five "W" questions (who, what, where, when, and why) and the "H" question (how). To get your message across effectively, put the most important information first. By stating "bottom line" information upfront, you're certain to hook the readers who really do have an interest in what you have to say.

If writing newsletter stories sounds like too daunting a task, consider hiring a freelance writer to produce the copy for you under your guidance. Good sources for finding freelance help include local professional advertising organizations, your local chamber of commerce, university journalism programs, and even the Yellow

Free Publicity

The media are always looking for interesting stories to fill space on a page or on the air, and people are always interested in services that can help make their lives easier. Keep your name out in front of them as much as you can by trying some of these less conventional strategies:

- ○ *Become an expert.* If you have an area of expertise or a special interest in a particular aspect of horticulture, let the local media know so they can call you when they need an expert opinion. (Example: You just took a pesticide class and the grub infestation is particularly bad this year. Don't be shy—alert the media!)
- ○ *Make a donation.* Donate some professional time—say, a month of mowing—to your local public TV station for an annual auction. Or you could donate a tool or other lawn-related item to be auctioned off.
- ○ *Offer a seminar.* Spread your knowledge by teaming up with local home and garden shops, garden clubs, and other organizations to give pointers on how to make your lawn look lush and beautiful. Don't worry about giving away trade secrets and losing business. There will be enough people there who won't have a clue what you're talking about, or might not have the inclination to put your ideas into practice. Then, bingo—you end up with more viable leads.
- ○ *Support your community.* Donate materials or time to help a local environmental group or garden club. Your benevolence will resonate throughout the community.
- ○ *Take up a cause.* Actively supporting environmental protection can put you in the spotlight. But avoid controversial issues and politics. Whichever side you take, you'll alienate the people who support the other side.

Pages. You can expect to pay $350 to $700 for a four-page newsletter, depending on the experience of the writer. You also could use a marketing firm, but that can be pretty expensive for a new business owner.

The standard size for a newsletter is letter-sized. It's usually produced in multiples of four pages, but there's absolutely no reason why you can't do a two-pager, which is a single sheet with type on the front and back. It's usually easy to come up with enough copy to fill a two-page newsletter, and it will keep your costs down since it can easily be produced on a photocopier and mailed in a No. 10 business envelope.

After the copy has been written, it has to be placed into position on the newsletter pages. There are a number of affordable software packages available to help you do this yourself. Many of them come with newsletter templates that allow you to type in headlines and paste in copy blocks, and the program does the copy fitting and formatting. A reasonably priced desktop package you can try is Microsoft Publisher Deluxe (retail $129.99). Microsoft Word also comes with a newsletter template, but don't forget that everyone else who owns Word may be using the same template.

It's perfectly acceptable to design your newsletter with all words and no artwork. But clip art is now so inexpensive and easy to use that it makes sense to buy an all-purpose clip art package that includes lawn and garden art. (Don't forget you can use the clip art on other promotional materials you create, too, including fliers.) A good clip art package to try is ClickArt Premiere Image Pak 300,000 from Broderbund, which retails for $29.95. In addition, the bundled Microsoft Office software package includes a nice selection of lawn and garden clip art you can use. And by the way, although photographs can really make a newsletter look great, don't use them if you're planning to photocopy it. The reproduction quality will be terrible, which will diminish your newsletter's appearance.

If you don't feel up to the task of designing your newsletter, hire a freelance designer to lay out the publication, or create a simple template you can use over and over. You can expect to pay up to $500 (or $30 to $60 per hour) for a designer's services.

Feature Articles

Feature stories are an excellent way to garner publicity for your business. What makes these articles such powerful and effective tools is the fact that they can be used to position you as an authority in your field. It's a great way to gain credibility in your field while building a solid reputation as a savvy businessperson.

Feature stories can run the gamut from informational articles to profiles about your company. The slant you take depends on the type of publication you're planning to submit the article to. For instance, a story on "The Top Ten Reasons to Hire a Lawn Care Professional" might be perfect for the features section of your daily newspaper. On the other hand, an article about your entrepreneurial talents or your successful business start-up might be more appropriate for the business section of your paper or a specialty business magazine.

Don't overlook the value of sharing your knowledge and insight with readers. The idea is to "wow" them with your expertise so they immediately think of you when they're ready to engage someone to take over the lawn care duties at their home. So write articles giving tips for cultivating a beautiful, lush lawn. Share stories about fertilizing disasters and how they can be fixed or avoided. Or report on the innovative and unusual landscaping you installed for the city's leading citizen. The possibilities are endless.

> **Bright Idea**
>
> If you're going after commercial business, you should consider packaging all of your promotional and sales materials in a media kit, which can be distributed to business prospects. Some of the items in the kit (which are usually organized in a pocket folder) may include a letter thanking the client for his or her interest, some background information about the business, copies of any articles you have been quoted in (or are the star of), a brochure or flier, and your qualifications (including chemical certifications).

Although feature articles can run anywhere from 800 to 2,500 words, depending on the publication, a reasonable length is 1,200 to 1,500 words. As with newsletters, you can use a freelance writer to "ghostwrite" or produce the articles under your byline. You can expect to pay a freelance ghostwriter $350 to $750 for a 1,200-word article.

Submitting Your Manuscript

The article manuscript should be on letter-sized white bond paper with one inch margins on all sides. Send the article with a pitch letter that briefly describes what the article is about and why it would appeal to the readers of the publication. Always remember to give information about how and where you can be reached.

Locating the right recipient for the article is a cinch. You can either call the magazine or newspaper to find out the name of the appropriate person, or check the publication's Web site for a list of editorial staff members. Never address your story to "Editor" or, worse yet, just the name of the publication. It's far less likely to get to the appropriate person that way. A few days after you've mailed the article, follow up with the editor by phone.

Home and Garden Show Promotions

For sheer numbers, there may be no better place to gain quick exposure for your business than a consumer home and garden show. These events attract hundreds or even thousands of homeowners—people who, by their presence alone, are announcing loudly and clearly that they're interested in the services you offer.

Home and garden shows are generally held in convention centers in large cities. For a fairly reasonable price, you can rent booth space in these shows. Then it's up to you to chat up prospective customers, cheerfully hand out your business card and services list, and otherwise lay the groundwork that will result in new business.

If you've ever been to a trade show of any kind before, you know that some companies set up elaborate booths with fancy graphics and high-tech lighting. But don't feel like you have to go this route, too. After all, you're a small-business owner, and as such, you're probably not in a position to drop thousands of dollars on a booth you'll use just a few times a year. So instead, put on a shirt with your company logo and accessorize it with a big smile. Once you start talking to people, no one's even going to notice your modest booth space with its 10- or 12-foot skirted table.

One thing they will notice, however, is any giveaway items you have. You definitely will want to spring for at least one novelty item since you'll be competing with other companies that offer the same kinds of products and services. Specialty items like pens, nail files, refrigerator magnets, and other gizmos that are personalized with the name and address of your business are great giveaways. The hope is, of course, that every time the prospect picks up the item, he or she will be reminded of your business and will one day call for an estimate.

Advertising specialty items (known as "trinkets and trash" in the biz) are surprisingly inexpensive. For example, 500 Bic Clic pens personalized with your company name might cost just $297. Or you could get 1,000 neon stick-up calendars for just $270. If an item—any item—can be imprinted, there's probably a specialty promotional company that carries it.

Prize drawings are an effective way to attract people to your booth. The prize should be something lawn care-related that would be perceived as valuable to this audience, like a month's worth of free mowing or one power raking. Prepare entry forms in advance (you can create them six to a page using your home computer, then have the pages photocopied at a quick print shop and cut into individual forms), and bring a big fishbowl or another container to collect them. Then when people come up to fill out the entry forms, start a conversation to find out whether they're in your target market, and if so, pitch them for all you're worth.

Even if you don't come away with any firm commitments from the people in attendance, you'll still have something very valuable as a result of your efforts: a fishbowl full of leads that you can use to send out direct mail advertising or a newsletter you've developed especially for this purpose.

Some of the major national home and garden shows in the United States are listed in the Appendix under "Home and Garden Shows."

Networking

You know the old saying: It's not what you know, but who you know. And the more people you know, the easier it will be to drum up new business.

Two extremely valuable networking sources are your local chamber of commerce and Rotary Club. These organizations consist of both small- and large-business owners, and encourage their members to exchange ideas, support each other's businesses, and barter services. The cost to join either organization is reasonable, and you can quickly build a reputation as a caring and reputable business owner by becoming involved in the groups' public service activities. More important, you can network on a regular basis with other business owners who may need residential or commercial lawn care services themselves, or who may know someone who does.

Finally, professional lawn care service organizations are a good place to meet other business owners and share tips and techniques. Many of the national organizations have regional chapters that hold regular meetings.

12

The Green
Stuff

Well, you've certainly accomplished a lot
if you've made it this far. Hopefully, the prospects of making a
go at this lawn service gig are looking pretty promising to you
right now. But there's one teensy little thing you still have to
work out—something that can mean the difference between

▲

soaring success and abysmal failure. We're talking, of course, about the ongoing financial management of your business.

Did you just turn pale and look heavenward for help? If so, you're not alone. Many of us make certain career choices because we're not as interested in or adept at other ones. So while you can turn grass a mean shade of green and sculpt it like an artist, you may not be comfortable with balance sheets and cash flow statements. This doesn't mean you can't learn how to do it, of course. But at the very least you need to know how much money is coming in and how much is going out, and to do that you need to have patience, perseverance, and maybe a software package or two to keep those numbers on your financial statements in the black.

Anyone who's been in this business for a while will tell you that one of its main challenges (aside from avoiding nitrogen burnout and dodging pesky dogs) is being able to stash away enough "scratch" during your busy season to keep you afloat during the lean days of winter. Even if you live in a part of the country where winters are mild, such as Florida, you'll still experience times when revenues are slimmer. (For instance, some of those snowbirds who fly down from the northern states may be tempted to do some of the yardwork themselves, thus impacting your revenue stream.) Planning for such eventualities is key to weathering the slow times in this seasonal industry.

In this chapter, we'll discuss the tools of financial management and how to calculate the amount of money you'll need to carry you through the off-season.

Income and Operating Expenses

In Chapter 5, we mentioned the value of a good accountant who can help you through the wonders of corporate bookkeeping. But you still must know enough about your own business situation to understand what he or she is doing to keep you honest in the eyes of the IRS and your creditors.

One tool you'll need is a simple income/operating expenses worksheet like the one on page 129 that will help you estimate your monthly expenses. The statement shows the operating costs for two hypothetical lawn service businesses—one whose owner handles all the work alone, and another whose owner has two part-time employees. Not all the expenses shown will apply to you, but it gives a rundown of the typical expenses a lawn care service professional can expect to incur.

Phone/Utilities

Assuming you have a business telephone line, you can note the total cost of the bill. Your cellular phone bill should be included in this amount if the phone is used strictly for business.

If you decide to use your home phone as your business line when you start out, estimate only the cost of the business calls you expect to make, since Uncle Sam won't allow you to deduct the entire phone bill on your business tax return. A word of advice: Keep a handwritten log of business calls that you can compare against your phone bill every month. The IRS usually requires written records for any expenses you deduct, and it will be much easier to determine which calls are legitimate business expenses if you have a log to refer to.

Postage

As mentioned in Chapter 9, you may want to do a mass mailing a few times a year to drum up new prospects. Estimate your postage costs here. Also, if you anticipate having any monthly shipping charges, include those, too.

Wages

Depending on your situation, you may have part- or full-time workers to help you with lawn care or clerical tasks in the office. Lawn care service owners generally pay their employees a few dollars over minimum wage, although a few of the owners Entrepreneur contacted said they paid $10 or more in order to attract and keep top-notch help.

Advertising

Include the cost of fliers and other advertising you may decide to do. Yellow Pages advertising would also go here.

Insurance

Using the worksheet on page 49 in Chapter 5, tally up the amount of insurance you plan to carry, including the cost to insure the truck or van you'll use to transport yourself, your crew, and your equipment to job sites. As with the phone expenses, you should only note business-specific expenses. If you also use your vehicle to transport the kids to a ballgame or to go shopping, you'll have to estimate what percentage of the vehicle is actually used for your business, then apply that to your insurance cost to arrive at a useable number. One reliable way to do this that the IRS will find acceptable is to keep a simple mileage log. Office supply stores sell mileage log books that are small enough to stash in your glove compartment or a pocket of your visor. Make sure you jot down both business and personal mileage every time you get behind the wheel, or your records won't be acceptable to the IRS.

Transportation/Maintenance

Keeping your equipment in good working order is paramount since you'll be out of business if it's not reliable and ready to go when you are. Tally up the cost of regular tune-ups for both your power equipment and your vehicle, then add in an amount to cover regular maintenance like oil changes and spark plug replacement. Then add in the estimated cost of gasoline, windshield wiper fluid, and any travel-related costs, as well as vehicle payments if appropriate.

Office Supplies

This includes all the paper clips, stationery, business cards, and other supplies you need to do business every day. Obviously, some expenses like business printing won't be incurred every month, so use the figures you got when you priced your business cards and divide by 12. This number gets added to the other costs you've estimated for the month.

Online Service Fees

This one is easy to predict since you'll sign up for service at a set price. The average is $15 to $20 a month, but you can find bargain rates that are lower, as well as some that are higher. Web hosting charges, which average around $15 per month, also should be plugged in here.

Other Miscellaneous Expenses

Other incidentals like herbicides for spraying cracks in the sidewalk or trash bags for your clipping collection are added in here. Adding 10 percent to your bottom line total to cover incidentals usually works well.

Receivables

Here's where the fun begins. Hopefully, the money you receive from your clients will offset all the operating expenses you just read about and leave you with a little change to jingle in your pocket that will carry you through the entire year. But the only way you'll know where you stand is by keeping careful records of your receivables.

We've provided a receivables worksheet on page 130 that you can use to track the fruits of your labor. You can either reproduce the sheet provided there, or customize your own using a standard accountant's columnar pad available at any office supply store. These pads come with two to 12 or more columns to keep your accounting tidy. Usually, a six-column pad will do the job nicely. It's low-tech, but it works for people who are not computer-literate or too busy to learn. If you decide to invest in an accounting software package (discussed in further detail later in this chapter), you can log your receivables right on your computer and always have a running total available.

> ## Smart Tip
>
> **Tip...**
>
> If you'd like to offer customers the convenience of paying with a major credit card, you'll need to establish a merchant account through a bank or an independent sales organization (ISO) before you can buy a credit card imprinting device. But be forewarned: Banks and ISOs generally view small businesses as risky and may not be willing to grant you merchant status.

Paying the Piper

Of course, before you can line your pockets with silver, you'll have to bill your clients regularly. You'll find a sample invoice you can adapt to your specifications on page 131. All the lawn care professionals we spoke to said they bill monthly, and most use some kind of business software to do the job. No matter how you bill, make sure you get those invoices mailed out at the same time each month, like around the 1st or the 15th. In addition to keeping your cash flow *flowing*, sending bills on a regular schedule will get your customers accustomed to seeing your bill at a certain time, and hopefully, they'll work it into their monthly budgets.

High-Tech Bookkeeping Solutions

Accounting and business software has become so user-friendly and affordable that practically anyone can use it, including people who are financially challenged. The hands-down choice of the lawn care pros we interviewed was QuickBooks by Intuit. The Pro version retails for $250 and allows you to create invoices, track receivables, write checks, pay bills, and more. It also interfaces with Microsoft Word, Excel, and other software. Another plus: Data from QuickBooks can also be imported directly into income tax preparation packages like Turbo Tax if you're brave enough to do

Smart Tip

Tip...

A handshake is the preferred "contract" for most lawn care professionals. But if you'll be doing large-scale commercial work, you should draw up a written contract that spells out your responsibilities and payment terms. Under the Uniform Commercial Code, contracts for the sale of services or goods in excess of $500 must be in writing to be legally enforceable.

your own business or personal taxes (*not* recommended if your tax situation is complex). Both of these are available at most office supply and computer stores.

Another popular accounting package you might like to try is Peachtree Complete Accounting. It retails for $270 and is available online from computer stores like CompUSA (www.compusa.com).

One of the best reasons to use accounting software is because it prevents inadvertent math errors. All you have to do is plug in the correct numbers and they're crunched appropriately.

Where the Money Is

Now you have all your ducks in a row. Your business plan is exemplary, and you have solid evidence that your community or metropolitan area has the well-heeled economic base necessary to support your fledgling business. So financing should be a snap, right?

In your dreams. Small-business owners sometimes discover it's pretty hard to find a bank willing to work with them. This is usually because the megarich banks are a lot more interested in funding large companies that need lots of capital. They're also leery about dealing with one-person and start-up companies. So it may be hard to find the financing you need to buy reliable mowing equipment.

One way around this problem is to shop around to find a bank that will actually welcome the opportunity to work with you. "Small-business owners usually do better by selecting a bank with a community banking philosophy," says Robert Sisson, vice president and commercial business manager of Citizens Bank in Sturgis, Michigan, and author of *Show Me the Money* (Adams Media, 2000). "These are the banks that support their communities and function almost as much as a consultant as a bank."

You probably already have a pretty good idea who the smaller banking players are in your community. Start by checking out their annual reports, which are usually readily available at branch offices, for clues about their financial focus and business outlook. Important clue: Institutions that support minority- and women-owned businesses as well as small businesses are likely to be more willing to help *your* small business (even if you personally are not a minority or a woman). Next, look for information about the

Take Some Credit

Financing your lawn care business start-up with your personal credit cards can save you both the hassle of applying for a bank loan and the hefty costs that can be associated with it. Of course, the downside is that you'll probably pay interest rates of as much as 24.9 percent. So if you decide to use plastic, use a card with the lowest interest rate. Keep checking your mailbox for low rate offers. There are even zero percent offers out there, which is much appreciated by business owners who are just starting out.

If your credit is good, you may be able to obtain a separate small-business line of credit through your credit card company. This allows you to borrow as much as $25,000 with no other costs than an application fee and at a rate that's probably a lot less than what your bank would charge for a similar line of credit. American Express is one company that offers such a small-business line of credit.

Tapping into the equity in your home is another possible way to secure funding. Banks now offer up to 125 percent equity loans. Just remember that your house is the collateral for the loan, and if the business doesn't do well and you can't make the payments, you could lose your home. Check with an accountant before getting your hopes up of using such a loan to start up the business because there are fairly tight restrictions on how you can use home equity funds. You don't want to break the rules, either inadvertently or on purpose, both because the bank could call in the whole loan if you're thought to be using the funds in an unapproved way, and because Uncle Sam is watching.

number of loans banks make to small companies. That's a pretty good indicator of their community commitment. Finally, study their overall business mix and the industries they serve.

While it's not impossible to find a big bank that will welcome you into the financial fold, it's actually far more likely that warm welcome will come from a smaller financial institution.

"Small banks traditionally are better for small businesses because they're always looking for ways to accommodate these customers," says Wendy Thomas, senior business consultant at the Michigan Small Business Development Center at the One Stop Capital Shop in Detroit. "Small banks are simply more willing to deal with small-business concerns and are more sensitive to issues like the need for longer accounts receivable periods." Visit www.entrepreneur.com/bestbanks for a list of small-business banks.

Uncle Sam to the Rescue

Even if you do find a bank that's friendly to small business, you may still have trouble establishing credit or borrowing money as a start-up business. Banks both large and small are always more reluctant to part with their cash when the business owner doesn't have a proven track record.

That's where agencies like the Small Business Administration (SBA) can help. It offers a number of free services to small-business owners, including counseling and training seminars on topics like business plan and marketing plan development. The idea is to help the owner understand what the bank will want from him or her before ever setting foot inside the front door.

The SBA also offers a number of different loan programs, counseling, and training. For more information, check the SBA's Web site at www.sba.com, or call the answer desk at (800) 827-5722.

Do-It-Yourself Financing

Even with all the traditional financing options out there, some newly established lawn care business owners prefer to use creative financing methods instead. Albert T. in Detroit used a profit-sharing check from his full-time job with one of the automotive companies to buy some of his equipment, then financed his mowers. Others, like Lowell P. in Stanwood, Washington, use windfalls like income tax refunds to get started. Some, like Nathan B. in Sykesville, Maryland, whip out their plastic to buy the machinery, staplers, and other goodies that make the business go, then secure a vehicle loan to pay for their truck. Still others rely on loans from friends and family.

Whichever way you go, make sure the transaction is handled in a professional, businesslike manner. This is particularly important if you borrow from loved ones. Always sign a promissory note that details repayment terms and an equitable interest rate. Nothing can destroy a tight-knit family faster than a broken promise of repayment or a misunderstanding about how it will be handled. Your new business is important, but your family is precious. Protect it just like you would protect your business assets.

If you use your personal credit cards, watch your expenses closely. You can easily put yourself thousands of dollars in debt if you're not careful. Start out with the bare minimum whenever possible so your business will have a chance to grow and prosper without the specter of debt hanging over.

Income/Operating Expenses

Here are sample income/operating expenses statements for two hypothetical lawn services that reflect typical operating costs for this industry. The Yard Man is a part-time business that services 20 clients per week. Mowing Masters handles 40 weekly clients and has two part-time employees (20 hours per week apiece). You can compute your own projected income and expenses using the worksheet provided on page 129.

The Yard Man

Projected monthly income	**$3,200**
Projected monthly expenses	
Phone (office and cell)	$40
Postage	7
Wages	
Advertising	
Insurance (commercial auto)	200
Gasoline, other maintenance	250
Self-storage unit	109
Accounting services	
Misc. expenses (stationery and office supplies; garbage bags)	50
Loan repayment	200
Online service	20
Web hosting	
Total Expenses	**$876**
Projected Income/Expense Total	**$2,324**

Mowing Masters

Projected monthly income	**$8,000**
Projected monthly expenses	
Phone (office and cell)	$65
Postage	14
Wages	1,600
Advertising	75
Insurance (commercial auto)	200
Gasoline, other maintenance	350
Self-storage unit	219
Accounting services	50
Misc. expenses (stationery and office supplies; garbage bags)	50
Loan repayment	500
Online service	20
Web hosting	20
Total Expenses	**$3,163**
Projected Income/Expense Total	**$4,837**

Income/Operating Expenses Worksheet

Projected monthly income		$
Projected monthly expenses	$	
Phone (office and cell)		
Postage		
Wages		
Advertising		
Insurance (commercial auto)		
Gasoline, other maintenance		
Self-storage unit		
Accounting services		
Misc. expenses (stationery and office supplies; garbage bags)		
Loan repayment		
Online service		
Web hosting		
Total Expenses		$
Projected Income/Expense Total		$

Receivables Worksheet

Receivables 200x

Date Posted	Client	Amount	Check #	Balance Due

Sample Invoice

MOWING MASTERS

25771 Regal Drive
Kissimmee, Florida 34741
(555) 555-5555

Invoice

July 30, 200x   Terms: Net 30

Sold to:
David Mower
49855 Petrucci Dr.
Lake Buena Vista, FL 55555

Mowing and edging service for July 200x
4 weeks @ $20 per cut $80
Fertilizing (3rd seasonal application) @ $31/application $31

Total $111

Thank you!

13

Your Green
Piece on Earth

In Chapter 1, we mentioned with unabashed optimism all the opportunities that exist in the lawn care service industry for hard-working, dedicated, and disciplined small-business owners like you. Of course, all of these opportunities also require a stash of cash and a liberal dose of business savvy.

▲

But for the most part, enthusiasm for the job and the tenacity to go the distance are just as crucial for success as a healthy cash infusion.

It is our hope at Entrepreneur that all your plans and hard work pay off and you enjoy both satisfaction and longevity in your newly chosen career. But even as we wish you the best as you embark on this exciting new venture, we must acknowledge that every new business owner faces pitfalls that could threaten his or her existence.

Business by the Numbers

According to D&B, there are 11 million small businesses (defined as businesses with one to 500 employees) in the United States, and they employ more than half of the private workforce. What's more, 60 percent all new businesses begin as home-based ventures, according to the U.S. Department of Labor.

So far, so good. But let's do a reality check here. A lot of these small businesses don't survive the very first year.

Why Businesses Fail

Surveys by organizations like the SBA have shown that the reasons for these failures are numerous. Business failures in the service industry can occur due to poor customer relations, underpriced services, insufficient insurance, market conditions (such as competition, increases in the cost of doing business. and so on), financing and cash flow problems, poor planning, mismanagement, and a host of other problems.

> **Beware!**
> The Small Business Administration reports that too many small-business owners in financial straits don't call for help until it's too late to salvage their company. Don't fall into this trap. If you ever need help, call the SBA, which can provide advice and direction, or act as a loan guarantor. There's no charge for this service, and it could save everything you've worked for.

That's why we strongly recommend that you hire professionals like attorneys, bookkeepers, accountants, and employees to assist you in the proper management and operation of your business. Because no matter how enthusiastic, bright, and determined you may be, you're probably not an expert in every field, and your time will only stretch so far. In the beginning, it can be pretty hard to part with the cash to pay those professional fees, but in the long run, it's worth it because this kind of help will allow you to focus your attention on the services you do and like best.

By the way, the outlook for success in your new business isn't totally grim.

Statistics suggest that the longer you're in business, the better your chances are of staying afloat. In fact, D&B reports that 70 percent of small businesses are still in business eight and a half years later. That's not a bad outlook considering the capricious nature of both consumers and the U.S. economy.

Weathering the Storm

Nearly every lawn care professional who agreed to be interviewed for this book readily admitted there were things he would do differently if it were possible to start again. For instance, Steve M. in Mendota Heights, Minnesota, who assumed control of an established company that came complete with 60 clients, said he should have done more due diligence before agreeing to the sale. Not only did he feel he paid too much for the business, but he soon found out that the age and condition of the equipment that came along with it had been misrepresented. He solved some of his early operating problems by replacing the equipment, but "it was a hard decision to spend the dough," he says.

Nathan B. in Sykesville, Maryland, who now has 200 customers (150 of whom are mowing accounts), believes he should have paid more attention to certain business details. "A mission statement would have been extremely helpful," he admits. "I also should have created more standardized business systems so the company could have run on its own more smoothly. I think it might have helped to create a manual with specific guidelines for every aspect of the business."

Stat Fact

According to a study released by the Small Business Administration in 1999, about 45 percent of businesses filing for bankruptcy had one or no employees.

Lowell P. in Stanwood, Washington, wishes he had acquired the business acumen he needed sooner. He also would have liked to have started earlier in life, both because he probably could have avoided hurting his back if he was younger, and because he would have been able to expand the business faster. "After eight years, I should be trying to put a third crew on instead of just now starting to put on a second crew," Lowell says.

Mike A. in Renner, South Dakota, who has had his part-time business for three years, also believes he should have started his business earlier. He figures that by beginning while he was in his 20s rather than his late 30s, he, too, could now have multiple crews and more time to manage the business instead of going out on jobs himself. He also thinks he should have moved beyond the boundaries of his own community, where there are 28 lawn care companies listed in the phone book.

"Collections have always been hard—definitely the hardest part of this business," Albert T. in Detroit says. "The check's always in the mail."

Although there are things they could have done better, each of these intrepid entrepreneurs relied on creative thinking, hard work and good old-fashioned determination to meet whatever challenges faced him. Obviously, this is a strategy that works. These small-business owners not only survived that scary first year; many are prospering now.

Was it a miracle that they persevered in the face of economic uncertainties, weathering setbacks, and other pressures? Definitely not. It's due more to having the right stuff and knowing how to use it. It's also due to being willing to "go the extra mile" and provide exceptional customer service.

"I have a whole collection of notes from customers thanking me because their lawn is so beautiful," Lowell P. says. "There's a lot of personal satisfaction in this business because I have the immediate reward of seeing my work when it's done. I like knowing my customers are going to come home and go, 'Wow!' "

All in a Day's Work

Customers aren't the only ones who say "wow" in this business. Sometimes, the owners themselves are confronted with unexpected situations that leave them shaking their heads.

Unexpected Company

Albert T. was out mowing one day when a man in the yard next door kept staring at him. When he shut off the mower, the neighbor asked him if he had seen a snake. Albert assured the guy that he hadn't and went back to cutting. But when he began working under a tree, he happened to look up and saw an eight-foot boa constrictor wrapped around a branch above his head. "It was the guy's pet," Albert says. "I was lucky it wasn't hungry—it already had a mouse or something in its [throat]!"

Making the Grade

Part-time business owner Bill V. in Urbana, Illinois, once had a close encounter of the absurd kind when he was mowing on a slope. While riding his Dixon Zero

Turning Radius mower, which has a rear-mount engine, he misjudged the steepness of the slope and accidentally popped a wheelie.

"The mower got stuck in the ground with the blades in operation and me still on it," Bill says. "I had to turn off the blades and the mower before I could slide over the seat and get off. Since then, I only push-mow that slope!"

House Call

One reason some lawn service entrepreneurs get into the business is because they enjoy the great outdoors. One of Nathan B.'s employees took this appreciation for nature to new heights when he was mowing around a pool one day. "Suddenly, he grabbed one of those nets you use to fish stuff out of the pool and rescued a baby rabbit from the water," Nathan says. "He even did CPR on it."

The heroic gesture worked—the bunny survived none the worse for wear and Nathan's employee nonchalantly went back to mowing.

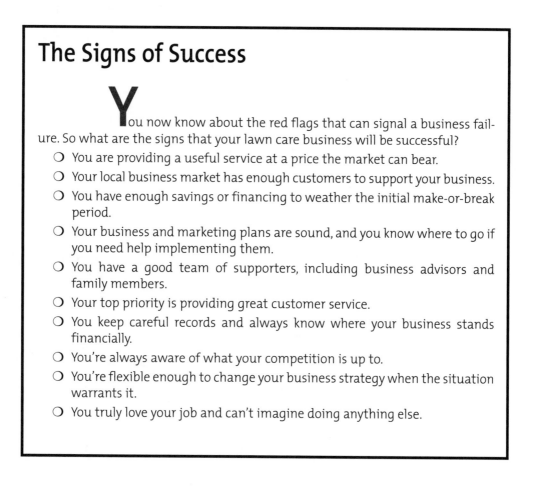

The Signs of Success

You now know about the red flags that can signal a business failure. So what are the signs that your lawn care business will be successful?

- ○ You are providing a useful service at a price the market can bear.
- ○ Your local business market has enough customers to support your business.
- ○ You have enough savings or financing to weather the initial make-or-break period.
- ○ Your business and marketing plans are sound, and you know where to go if you need help implementing them.
- ○ You have a good team of supporters, including business advisors and family members.
- ○ Your top priority is providing great customer service.
- ○ You keep careful records and always know where your business stands financially.
- ○ You're always aware of what your competition is up to.
- ○ You're flexible enough to change your business strategy when the situation warrants it.
- ○ You truly love your job and can't imagine doing anything else.

▲

Your Formula for Success

It's easy to see that the kind of resourcefulness and flexibility exhibited by the owners mentioned here and throughout this book are the hallmarks of a lawn service professional. It's also worth repeating that hard work and single-minded determination are other traits these owner/operators share that have contributed to their success.

Now it's time for you to turn green grass into cold cash. Best of luck in your new venture!

Appendix
Lawn Care
Resources

Advertising Specialty Items

Specialty Promotions Unlimited, 43 Park Dr., Mt. Kisco, NY 10549, (800) 539-3751, www.specprom.com, info@specprom.com

Attorney Referrals

American Bar Association, Service Center, 541 N. Fairbanks Ct., Chicago, IL 60611, (312) 988-5522

Find an Attorney, The Trenton Group, (888) 544-9800, www.find anattorney.com

Martindale-Hubbell Law Directory, 121 Chanlon Rd., New Providence, NJ 07974, (800) 627-8463, fax: (908) 464-3553, www.martindale.com, listings@martindale.com

Demographic Information

American Demographics, P.O. Box 10580, Riverton, NJ 08076-0580, (800) 529-7502, www.demographics.com

U.S. Census Bureau, www.census.gov

Employee Assistance

U.S. Department of Labor, ILAG Office of Public Affairs, 200 Constitution Ave. NW, Rm. N-2235, Washington, DC 20210, (202) 693-4770, www.dol.gov

Home and Garden Publications

Better Homes and Gardens, Meredith Corp., P.O. Box 37449, Boone, IA 50037-0449, (800) 374-4244, www.bhg.com

Flower & Garden Magazine, 51 Kings Highway W., Haddonfield, NJ 08033, (800) 444-1054, e-mail: kcpublishing@earthlink.net,www.flowerandgardenmag.com

House & Garden, Condé Nast Publications Inc., Condé Nast Bldg., 4 Times Square, New York, NY 10036, (212) 286-2860, fax: (212) 286-4672, www.house-and-garden.com

Southern Living Garden Guide, P.O. Box 523, 2100 Lakeshore Dr., Birmingham, AL 35201, (800) 272-4101, www.southernliving.com

Home and Garden Shows

Cleveland Home & Garden Show, Expositions Inc., P.O. Box 550, Edgewater Dr., Cleveland, OH 44107-0550, (216) 529-1300, fax: (216) 529-0311, www.expoinc.com, e-mail: expoinc@expoinc.com

GMC Builders Home & Detroit Flower Show, Building Industry Association of Southeastern Michigan, 30375 Northwestern Hwy., Farmington Hills, MI 48334, (248) 737-4477

GMC Southern California Home & Garden Show, DMG World Media, (800) 442-7469, www.dmgworldmedia.com

International Lawn, Garden & Power Equipment Exposition, Sellers Expositions, 222 Pearl St., #300, New Albany, IN 47150, (800) 558-8767, (812) 949-9200, fax: (812) 949-9600, http://expo.mov.org

Texas Home & Garden Show, Atlantic Communications, 1635 W. Alabama, Houston, TX 77006, (713) 529-1616, (800) 654-1480, fax: (713) 821-1169, e-mail: info@ieiem.com, www.texashomeandgarden.com

Lawn and Landscape Industry Conferences and Trade Shows

Central Environmental Nursery Trade Show (CENTS), The Ohio Nursery and Landscape Association, 72 Dorchester Sq., Westerville, OH 43081-3350, (800) 825-5062, fax: (800) 860-1713, www.onla.org

Florida Nursery & Allied Trades Show, Florida Nurserymen and Growers Association, 1533 Park Center Dr., Orlando, FL 32835, (407) 295-7994, fax: (407) 295-1619, e-mail: info@fnga.org, www.fnga.org

Green Industry Conference, Professional Lawn Care Association of America, 1000 Johnson Ferry Rd. NE, Ste. C-135, Marietta, GA 30068-2112, (800) 458-3466, e-mail: plcaa@plcaa.org,www.plcaa.org

Green Industry Expo, c/o Professional Lawn Care Association of America, 1000 Johnson Ferry Rd. NE, Ste. C-135, Marietta, GA 30068-2112, (770) 973-2019, fax: (770) 578-6071,e-mail: info@gieonline.com, www.gieonline.com

International Lawn, Garden & Power Equipment Exposition, Sellers Expositions, 222 Pearl St., #300, New Albany, IN 47150, (800) 558-8767, (812) 949-9200, fax: (812) 949-9600, http://expo.mow.org

Mid Am Trade Show, 1000 N. Rand Rd., #214, Wauconda, IL 60084-1188, (847) 526-2010, fax: (847) 526-3993, e-mail: mail@midam.org, www.midam.org

Lawn and Landscape Industry Trade Publications

Grounds Maintenance, P.O. Box 12914, Overland Park, KS 66282-2914, (800) 441-0294, fax: (913) 967-1903, www.grounds-mag.com

Landscape Management, Advanstar Communications Inc., 7500 Old Oak Blvd., Cleveland, OH 44130, (800) 736-3665, fax: (440) 891-2575, www.landscapemanagement.net

Lawn & Landscape Magazine, G.I.E. Inc., 4012 Bridge Ave., Cleveland, OH 44113, (216) 961-4130, fax: (216) 916-0364, www.lawnandlandscape.com

PRO Magazine, Cygnus Business Media, 1233 Janesville Ave., Fort Atkinson, WI 52538, (920) 563-6388, fax: (920) 563-1699, www.promagazine.com

Turf Magazine, P.O. Box 449, St. Johnsbury, VT 05819, (800) 422-7147, fax: (802) 748-1866, www.turfmagazine.com

Lawn Care Equipment Manufacturers

Exmark Manufacturing Co. Inc., Industrial Park NW, P.O. Box 808, Beatrice, NE 68310-0808, (402) 223-6300, (402) 223-6384, www.exmark.com

Honda Power Equipment Group, 4900 Marconi Dr., Alpharetta, GA 30005-8847, (800) 426-7701, fax: (678) 339-2670, www.hondapowerequipment.com

John Deere, Deere & Co., One John Deere Pl., Moline, IL 61265, (800) 537-8233, www.johndeere.com

RedMax, Komatsu Zenoah America Inc., 4344 Shackleford Rd., #500, Norcross, GA 30093, (800) 291-8251, fax: (770) 381-5150, www.redmax.com, e-mail: sales@red max.com

Scag Power Equipment, Division of Metalcraft of Mayville Inc., 1000 Metalcraft Dr., Mayville, WI 53050, (920) 387-0100, fax: (920) 387-0111, www.scag.com

Snapper Inc., 535 Macon St., McDonough, GA 30253, (800) 935-2967, (888) SNAPPER (commercial dealer locator number), e-mail: info@snapper.com, www.snapper.com

Stihl Inc., 536 Viking Dr., Virginia Beach, VA 23452, (800) GO-STIHL, www.stihl usa.com

The Toro Company, Commercial Division, 8111 Lyndale Ave. S., Bloomington, MN 55420, (952) 888-8801, www.toro.com

Lawn Care Service Owners

Albert's Lawn Service, Albert Towns Jr., 3984 Courville, Detroit, MI 48224, (313) 790-2623, e-mail: jrokhead@ameritech.net

Bill's Lawn Mowing, Bill Van Cleave, 1892 Liberty Ave., Urbana, IL 61802-7536, (217) 328-4674, e-mail: billvanc@home.com

The Cutting Crew, Steve Mager, 729 Mohican Ct., Mendota Heights, MN 55120, phone and fax (651) 457-0881, e-mail: omager4@aol.com

Green Thumb & Garden Care, Rick Quinby, 30572 Hollyberry Ln., Temecula, CA 92591, (909) 676-4130, e-mail: rickylyn@iinet.com

Ken Walkowski Lawn Maintenance, Ken Walkowski, 21750 Armada Center Rd., Armada, MI 48005, (810) 784-9294

Lawns of Leisure, Mike Ackerman, 25575 Stoneway Ave., Renner, SD 57055, (605) 543-6149, e-mail: greatlawn@svtv.com

Lowell's Lawn Service, Lowell Pitser, P.O. Box 443, Stanwood, WA 98292, (360) 387-8329, e-mail: lowellp@greatnorthern.net

Premier Lawn Services Inc., Nathan Bowers, 634 River Rd., Sykesville, MD 21784, (410) 489-4555, fax: (410) 489-4043, e-mail: nathanbowers@starpower.net

Tyler All Seasons Lawn & Tree Care, Chris Bryan, 1530 SSW Loop 323, #122, Tyler, TX 75701, (972) 877-7974, fax: (817) 577-0883, e-mail: tylerallseasons@aol.com

Magnetic Signs

A Magnetic Sign, Lettering Specialist Inc., P.O. Box 3410, 8020 N. Lawndale Ave., Skokie, IL 60076, (847) 674-3414, fax: (847) 674-9571, e-mail: signinfo@amagnetic sign.com, www.amagneticsign.com

The Graphic Guy, www.thegraphicguy.com

Sign Country, (409) 331-0199, fax: (409) 283-8383, e-mail: signcoungry@aol.com, http://signcountry.freeyellow.com/magnetic.html

Office Supplies, Forms, and Stationery

Amsterdam Printing & Litho Corp., Amsterdam, NY 12010-1899, (800) 833-6231, fax: (518) 843-5204

New England Business Service Inc., 500 Main St., Groton, MA 01471, (800) 225-6380, www.nebs.com (has contractor business forms catalog)

Office Depot, www.officedepot.com (Retail locations across the United States)

Office Max, www.officemax.com (Retail locations across the United States)

Paper Direct, 205 Chubb Ave., Lyndhurst, NJ 07071, (800) A-PAPERS

Rapidforms, 301 Grave Rd., Thorofare, NJ 08086-9499, (800) 257-8354, fax: (800) 451-8113

Staples, www.staples.com (Retail locations across the United States)

Professional Employer Organizations

SES, 2851 High Meadow Cr., Auburn Hills, MI 48326, (877) 737-5323, (248) 373-2000, fax: (248) 373-3697, www.sesworks.com

Professional Lawn and Landscape Associations

American Association of Nurserymen, 1250 I St., NW, #500, Washington, DC 20005, (202) 789-2900

Associated Landscape Contractors of America, 150 Elden St., #270, Herndon, VA 20170, (703) 736-9666, (800) 395-2522, fax: (703) 736-9668, www.alca.org

American Landscape Maintenance Association, P.O. Box 223218, Hollywood, FL 33022, (954) 925-7996

American Nursery and Landscape Association, 1250 I St., NW, #500, Washington, DC 20005, (202) 789-2900, www.anla.org

Association of Professional Landscape Designers, 1924 North Second St., Harrisburg, PA 17102, (717) 238-9780, fax: (717) 238-9985, www.alpd.com, info@apld.org

Independent Turf and Ornamental Distributors Association, 25250 Seeley Rd., Novi, MI 48375, (248) 476-5457, fax: (248) 476-5383, www.itoda.com, ITODAoffic@aol.com

Landscape Maintenance Association Inc., 1025 S. Sermoran Blvd., Winter Park, FL 32792-5511, (800) 797-1725, (407) 672-0633, fax: (407) 672-1369, e-mail: LMA@floridayards.com www.floridayards.com

Outdoor Power Equipment Distributors Association, 1900 Arch St., Philadelphia, PA 19103, (215) 564-3484 fax: (215) 963-9784,e-mail: opeda@fernley.com, www.opeda.org

*Professional Grounds Management Society,*120 Cockeysville Rd., #104, Hunt Valley, MD 21031, (410) 584-9754, (800) 609-7467, fax: (410) 584-9756, www.pgms.org

Professional Lawn Care Association of America, 1000 Johnson Ferry Rd., NE, Ste. C-135, Marietta, GA 80068-2112, (404) 977-5222

Professional Plant Growers Association, P.O. Box 27517, Lansing, MI 48909-0517, (517) 694-8560

Publishing Software

Microsoft Publisher, available from CompUSA retail outlets or www.compusa.com

Safety Equipment and Information

Contractor's Tools, P.J. Esberner and Associates Inc., 6252 Oakton St., Morton Grove, IL 60053, (800) 593-6095, (847) 583-0173, fax: (800) 544-3314, www.contractors tools.com

Occupational Safety and Health Administration (OSHA), U.S. Department of Labor, OSHA Office of Public Affairs, 200 Constitution Ave., NW, Rm. N-3649, Washington, DC 20210, (202) 693-1999, www.osha.gov

Software

CLIP, Sensible Software Inc., 9639 Doctor Perry Rd., #123, Ijamsville, MD 21754, (800) 635-8485, fax: (301) 874-3613, e-mail: sales@clip.com, www.clip.com

GroundsKeeper Pro, Adkad Technologies, 565 Herrick Rd., Delanson, NY 12053, (800) 586-4683, e-mail: info@adkad.com www.adkad.com,

Lawn Monkey, 1262 Don Mills Rd., #77, Toronto, ON M3B 2W7, CAN, (877) LAWN-MKY (toll-free in North America), (416) 640-6029 (Toronto and overseas), fax: (416) 984-8438,e-mail: sales@lawnmonkey.com, www.lawnmonkey.com

QuickBooks Pro, (888) 246-8848, www.quickbooks.com

Peachtree, Peachtree Software, 1505 Pavilion Pl., Norcross, GA 30093, (770) 724-4000, www.peachtree.com

Real Green, Real Green Systems, 8246 Goldie St., Walled Lake, MI 48390, (800) 422-7478, fax: (248) 360-5285, e-mail: realgreen@realgreen.com, www.realgreen.com

Route Rite, Performance Software Technologies, (800) 624-8244, (818) 889-1361, fax: (818) 889-4623, e-mail: routerite@earthlink.net, www.gopst.com

Tax Advice, Help, and Software

IRS, (800) TAX-FORM, fax-on-demand (703) 368-9694, www.irs.gov

Intuit TurboTax for Business, 2535 Garcia Ave., Mountain View, CA 94043, (650) 944-6000, www.intuit.com

Turfgrass Management Courses

Auburn University, College of Agriculture, 107 Comer Hall, Auburn University, AL 36849, (334) 844-2237, www.ag.auburn.edu

Clemson University, College of Agriculture, Forestry and Life Sciences, Clemson, SC 29634, (864)656-3311, http://virtual.clemson.edu/groups/CAFLS

Cornell University, New York State College of Agriculture & Life Sciences, 260 Roberts Hall, Ithaca, NY 14853, (607) 255-7635, www.cals.cornell.edu

Michigan State University, Department of Crop and Soil Sciences, 286 Plant and Soil Sciences, East Lansing, MI 48824-1325, (517) 353-3271, www.css.msu.edu

Ohio State University Turfgrass Science Program, College of Food, Agricultural and Environmental Sciences, 100 Agricultural Administration Bldg., 2120 Fyffe Rd., Columbus, OH 43210, http://cfaes.ohio-state.edu

Pennsylvania State University, College of Agricultural Science, 201 Agricultural Administration Bldg., University Park, PA 16802-2601, (814) 865-7522, www.psu.edu

University of Florida, College of Agricultural and Life Sciences, P.O. Box 110270, Gainesville, FL 32611, (352) 392-2251, e-mail: info@acprog.ifas.ufl.edu, www.acprog.ifas.ufl.edu

University of Georgia, College of Agricultural and Environmental Sciences, 102 Conner Hall, (706) 542-1611, fax: (706) 542-2130, e-mail: discover@arches.uga.edu, www.uga.edu/discover

University of Illinois at Urbana-Champaign, College of Agricultural, Consumer and Environmental Sciences, W-503 Turner Hall, 1102 S. Goodwin Ave., Urbana, IL 61801, (217) 333-2770, fax: (217) 244-3219 , e-mail: nres@uiuc.edu, www.nres.uiuc.edu

University of Kentucky, College of Agriculture, N-310 C Agricultural Science N. Bldg., Lexington, KY 40546-0091, (606) 257-3781, fax: (606) 257-3781, e-mail: jbuxton@ca.uky.edu, www.uky.edu/agriculture/Horticulture (Plant and Soil Science); www.uky.edu/Agriculture/LA (Landscape Architecture)

Web Hosting

Domain.com, www.domain.com

Prodigy Internet, http://pages.prodigy.net

Webhosting.com, www.webhosting.com

Yahoo!, www.yahoo.com

Work Shirts and Hats

New England Business Service Inc., 500 Main St., Groton, MA 01471, (800) 225-6380, www.nebs.com

The Cap Factory, 90 Windom St., Boston, MA 02134, (800) 222-HATS, (617) 783-1133, fax: (617) 783-3133, e-mail: mail@capfactory.com, www.capfactory.com

Glossary

Balancing weight: an inexpensive weight used on a lawn mower to help prolong mower life.

Clip art: simple graphics like drawings, photographs, and other artwork that can be inserted into documents—Microsoft Word and other word processing programs come with a small clip art collection as part of the main program.

Contingency fee: payment for legal services rendered as a percentage of a settlement amount (often 25 percent or higher).

dba: "doing business as," refers to your adoption of a pseudonym as the name of your business and is registered with your local or state government to make sure it's unique.

Ergonomic: designed for physical comfort and safety (for example, an ergonomic chair).

Feng shui: the ancient Chinese art of placement thought to improve the flow of chi, or energy, through the body, room, building, or landscape.

Freelancer: a self-employed person who works on a project or contract basis for businesses; also known as an independent contractor.

Hit: in Internet parlance, a successful retrieval of information from a Web site.

Independent contractor: see *freelancer.*

Litigator: an attorney who represents a client in a lawsuit.

Logo (or logotype): an identifying symbol used by companies in advertising or marketing; examples of logos are John Deere's leaping stag symbol and the Detroit Tigers' English "D" with its snarling tiger.

Mail merge: a computer software feature that merges a list of names and addresses into a form letter (this function is used for direct marketing and offered through word-processing programs like Word and WordPerfect).

Measuring wheel: a handheld device for pacing and measuring the dimensions of lawns and other areas.

Poly bag: a plastic sleeve that newspaper carriers (and others who deliver printed material) use to protect the paper from getting wet in inclement weather.

Portal: in Internet parlance, the electronic gateway users "pass through" to access Web sites.

Resolution: the clarity achieved by a printer or monitor, expressed as dpi.

Retainer: an amount of money paid in advance for services rendered at a later time.

Server: the computer that controls access to a network or peripherals (such as printers and disk drives).

Tag line: a slogan or block of descriptive text used to build audience recognition for a product (e.g., "got milk?").

Teaser: in advertising, copy or a headline meant to interest or hook the reader.

Telemarketing: using the telephone to generate new sales or leads.

Topiary: a shrub or tree cut into ornamental shapes; the fanciful "yard art" the title character creates in the movie "Edward Scissorhands" is an example of topiaries.

White finger: a form of Raynaud's disease caused by exposure to constant vibration, impairing circulation and causing fingers and toes to throb painfully after exposure to the cold (the affected digits appear tight, white, and shiny, then turn red as they warm up—sufferers often have a reduced ability to grip objects).

Index